ALLOWING TH
TO DEAL WITH 1ᴴᴱ ᴄREATURE

An Approach to the Spiritual Exercises
of Ignatius of Loyola

William A. Barry, S.J.

Paulist Press
New York/ Mahwah, N.J.

Library of Congress Cataloging-in-Publication Data

Barry, William A.
    Allowing the creator to deal with the creature: an approach to the spiritual exercises of Ignatius of Loyola / William A. Barry, S.J.
        p.   cm.
    Includes bibliographical references.
    ISBN 0-8091-3465-9 (pbk.)
    1. Ignatius, of Loyola, Saint, 1491-1556. Exercitia spiritualia. 2. Spiritual exercises. I. Title.
BX2179.L8B36   1994
248.3—dc20   94-16220
                                                                          CIP

Published by Paulist Press
997 Macarthur Boulevard
Mahwah, New Jersey 07430

Printed and bound in the
United States of America

TABLE OF CONTENTS

DEDICATION

IN GRATEFUL MEMORY OF
SISTER MARY AGNES REED, R.S.M.
WHO, AS SISTER MARY NATIVITY,
TAUGHT ME AT SACRED HEART GRAMMAR SCHOOL
WORCESTER, MASSACHUSETTS
AND WITH GREAT LOVE AND FIDELITY PRAYED FOR
AND CARED FOR ME
AND ALL THOSE WHOM SHE TAUGHT
UNTIL THE DAY OF HER DEATH
HOLY SATURDAY, APRIL 10, 1993

ACKNOWLEDGMENTS

Scripture taken from the New Revised Standard Version Bible, © 1989, Division of Christian Education of the National Council of the Churches of Christ in the United States of America.

Quotations from the *Spiritual Exercises* taken from George E. Ganss, *The Spiritual Exercises of Saint Ignatius. A Translation and Commentary* and used with the permission of the Institute of Jesuit Sources, St. Louis, MO. Permission is gratefully acknowledged.

The original form of chapter 1 was an address to an International Symposium on the *Spiritual Exercises* convened by the Institut d'Etudes Théologiques in Brussels in 1991 and published in French in *La pratique des Exercices Spirituels d'Ignace de Loyola: Actes du Symposium de Bruxelles du 1er au 6 avril 1991*. The original form of chapters 2, 3, 8 and 9 appeared in *Review for Religious*. A large section of chapter 6 first appeared as a chapter of *A Hunger for God* published by Sheed & Ward. Part of chapter 5 and the original form of chapter 7 appeared in *Human Development*. The original form of chapter 10 appeared in *The Way Supplement*. Permission to use these in revised form is gratefully acknowledged. I am grateful to Ave Maria for permission to reprint two sections of my *Finding God in All Things: A Companion to the Spiritual Exercises of St. Ignatius,* 1991. © 1993 by the New England Province of the Society of Jesus.

Preface

After Vatican Council II many religious orders and congregations began to reclaim their historical heritage, going back to their founders or foundresses to catch the original charism that led to the foundation of their orders or congregations. It was no different for the Society of Jesus. One discovery the Society made was that the *Spiritual Exercises* of their founder, Ignatius of Loyola, had originally been given to individuals, not groups. Prior to 1965 the notion of individually directed Exercises was almost unheard of, and had been unheard of, it seems, for more than a century. In living memory Jesuits and others knew nothing of a tradition of individually directed retreats. The *Spiritual Exercises* were preached to large groups of people, and they had an enormous impact in this form. So pervasive was this practice that there were some Jesuits who felt that the introduction of the individually directed retreat was an innovation, and perhaps an unhealthy one at that, another instance of the triumph of psychology in spiritual matters.

After 1965 Jesuits and others began to learn how to give the *Spiritual Exercises* to individuals. Training courses and programs proliferated. People in large numbers flocked to retreat houses to make individually directed retreats of varying lengths, up to the traditional thirty days. At first these people were largely men and women belonging to religious congregations and diocesan priests, but gradually the word spread among the laity and then to members of other Christian churches. Now there are a number of retreat houses in the United States that almost exclusively give directed retreats throughout the year. In addition, the rediscovery of the Ignatian heritage has led to the giving of the *Spiritual Exercises* to individuals and small groups while the retreatants carry on their ordinary daily lives. On any given day in the United States there are hundreds of people who are making the Exercises by praying for an hour and a half a day and seeing their director once a week while continuing to work a regular job and carry out their other daily tasks.

As a result of this recovery of the tradition, the *Spiritual Exercises* have taken on a new life in the church. Articles and books have appeared at a steady rate, climaxing in 1991 during the 500th anniversary of the birth of Ignatius. Since 1970 I have been engaged in giving the Exercises, in training directors of the Exercises and in writing on various aspects of Ignatian spirituality. During the Ignatian year I gave a series of lectures on the Exercises at Boston College, and this series was made into a book published in 1991 by Ave Maria Press, *Finding God in All Things: A Companion to the Spiritual Exercises of St. Ignatius.* That book tries to make the Exercises accessible to people with the hope that many more will want to try them out under direction. The present book has a different focus. I have reworked material already published in journals and added new material, all of which tries to show how I approach directing the Exercises. My hope is that the book will be helpful to directors, either to stimulate their own creative directing, or to be a foil against which they can joust to deepen our understanding and practice of using this tremendous tool given to the church by that sixteenth century religious genius, Ignatius of Loyola. I hope that the book may also be helpful to people who seek God, who want to let the Creator deal immediately with them. All my writing aims to be a help to people who hunger for God, to give God a chance to satisfy that hunger.

I have dedicated the book to Sister Mary Agnes Reed, R.S.M. who taught me in grade school and who always kept me in her heart and thoughts throughout her life. She died on Holy Saturday afternoon, 1993. As it turns out, I was putting the finishing touches on the first draft of this book as she lay dying and then died. Let her stand for all those dedicated Sisters of Mercy who helped shape my early years both intellectually and religiously. I am grateful to them all.

I want to take this opportunity to thank my father and sisters who so faithfully read my stuff and encourage me. Once again I am indebted to Marika Geoghegan, my good friend, who read the manuscript and gave me strong encouragement. My community of ten other Jesuits has been a great help to me since I became provincial two years ago. Without them I would not be able to do my job, nor would I have the time and energy to write. Moreover, they encourage me in my writing. I am especially grateful to William C. Russell, S.J. and William G. Devine, S.J. who read the first draft through very quickly and thoroughly, gave me helpful suggestions for improving it and expressed enthusiasm for the material. Finally, I take this opportunity to thank the past and present staff of the Center for Religious Development in Cambridge, Massachusetts who helped me to hone my approach to spiritual direction and to the direction of the Exercises and who encouraged me to write in those early days of learning how to direct the Exercises.

Laus Deo Semper!

1

ONE APPROACH:
"To Allow the Creator to Deal Immediately with the Creature and the Creature with His Creator and Lord"

In the Fifteenth Introductory Explanation to the *Spiritual Exercises* Ignatius urges the director to maintain an equilibrium with regard to the choices the retreatant faces. At the end of the paragraph he says: "Accordingly, the one giving the Exercises ought not to lean or incline in either direction but rather, while standing by like the pointer of a scale in equilibrium, to allow the Creator to deal immediately with the creature and the creature with his Creator and Lord" (n. 15). In this first chapter I want to outline how I approach directing the full Exercises, what is commonly called the "thirty-day Ignatian retreat." In other words, I want to present how I try "to allow the Creator to deal immediately with the creature and the creature with his Creator and Lord." To introduce my approach let me cite Gilles Cusson.

> We shall speak of the "integral" Exercises. This expression does not necessarily refer to the matter of time, that is, to the "thirty-day retreat." In fact, the making of the Exercises does not derive its value principally from the framework in which they are given, nor from the precision of details and their technical apparatus. Their authenticity is measured, instead, by the quality of the spiritual experience

which they foster, by their helping the retreatants to prepare themselves for the salutary encounter with God, in Christ.[1]

This strong statement echoes my own convictions that the *Spiritual Exercises* are a method of encountering God's action in our universe in an ordered progression, such that people who have the prerequisites and desires can let God strip them of their inordinate affections so that they can find God's will and thus become more and more attuned to God's salvific intention in creating this universe. Ignatius himself puts the purpose of his "spiritual exercises" as "to overcome oneself, and to order one's life, without reaching a decision through some disordered affection" (n. 21). For Ignatius, union with God meant union with a God who is always actively bringing about God's reign in this universe. Union with God meant ordered desires and action.[2]

In this chapter I will try to describe as succinctly as possible my own practice of giving the full *Spiritual Exercises,* a practice which has evolved over a period of about twenty years of directing individuals in retreats of varying lengths both in the city and in country retreat houses. The clientele has also varied from Jesuit novices and tertians to scholastics, sisters, Catholic and non-Catholic lay people, ministers and priests. My approach has been honed in peer group supervision with other directors. My approach has also undoubtedly been affected by my training as a clinical psychologist and my work as a training supervisor of spiritual directors and, of course, by my upbringing in the United States of America as the son of immigrant Irish parents. It remains to be seen whether and how this approach fits with the approaches of Jesuits and others from widely different cultures. I present my own approach with the hope that others will find it helpful, if only as a foil against which to test their own approaches.

The Principle and Foundation

I assume that the Exercises will be profitable for people according to the depth of their desires, a topic which we will take up explicitly in chapter 2. Those who are ready for the full Exercises must, I believe, have strong desires to develop and deepen their relationship with God. Such desires, if they are real, are based on strong, positive experiences of God, experiences which I have come to call the affective Principle and Foundation. It may help to understand my meaning if I first describe people who do not have such positive experiences of God. These are the fearful, scrupulous people whose image of God seems to be one of a tyrant. The British psychoanalyst Henry Guntrip notes:

> It is a common experience in psychotherapy to find patients who fear and hate God, a God who, in the words of J. S. Mackenzie, "is always snooping around after sinners," and who "becomes an outsize of the threatening parent.... The child grows up fearing evil rather than loving good; afraid of vice rather than in love with virtue."[3]

Pierre Favre, one of the founding members of the Society of Jesus, seems to have been in this condition when Ignatius first met him in Paris. Only after four years was Pierre ready for the full Exercises, after much patient spiritual direction by Ignatius. What the Favres of this world need in order to desire closeness to God and detachment from their inordinate desires is an experience of the enjoyment of God described by the psychiatrist J. S. Mackenzie.

> The *enjoyment of God* should be the supreme end of spiritual technique; and it is in that enjoyment of God that we feel not only saved in the Evangelical sense, but safe: we are conscious of belonging to God, and

hence are never alone; and, to the degree we have
these two, hostile feelings disappear. . . . In that relationship Nature seems friendly and homely; even its
vast spaces instead of eliciting a sense of terror speak
of the infinite love; and the nearer beauty becomes
the garment with which the Almighty clothes
Himself.[4]

Such experiences of the "enjoyment of God" elicit the
desire to get to know God and to let one's life be governed by
one's relationship with God.

Another way to describe this affective Principle and
Foundation would be to point to experiences of desiring "we
know not what," experiences of great well-being accompanied
by a yearning for Mystery itself. Sebastian Moore describes
such experiences and then explains them as experiences of being
desired into being by God, experiences of our creation which
immerse us in the great desire of the universe for the consum-
mation of God's own intention for the universe and for each one
of us.[5] C. S. Lewis calls this desire "Joy,"[6] an intense longing
which is distinguished from other longings by two things. "In
the first place, though the sense of want is acute and even
painful, yet the mere wanting is felt to be somehow a delight. . . .
This hunger is better than any other fullness; this poverty better
than all other wealth." Secondly, we can be mistaken about the
object of the desire, as Lewis himself was for a good part of his
early life. Lewis concludes:

It appeared to me therefore that if a man diligently
followed this desire, pursuing the false objects until
their falsity appeared and then resolutely abandoning
them, he must come out at last into the clear knowledge that the human soul was made to enjoy some
object that is never fully given — nay, cannot even

be imagined as given — in our present mode of sub-
jective and spatio-temporal experience.[7]

I believe that Ignatius spells out the implications of such an
experience in the First Principle and Foundation.[8]

When people have such an affective Principle and
Foundation, they desire to be united with God and to know
God's dreams for themselves and for the universe. Before I take
on someone for the full Exercises, I try to ascertain that he or
she has had sufficient positive experiences of God so that this
desire is present. In the first couple of days of the retreat I suggest exercises that will bring back to memory these experiences
of being desired into existence and kept in existence by a loving
Creator who has a dream for the person. Psalms such as 8, 104,
or 139 are proposed for prayer. I often suggest a day of prayer in
which the person asks God to reveal her personal salvation history. After expressing the desire for such a personal revelation,
she recalls a person, a place or an incident of early childhood
and then lets the memories rise almost like free association,
trusting that among the influences on her memories will be
God's Holy Spirit. In other periods of prayer on the same day
she can take up later periods of her life. The purpose is that she
experience anew and in depth God's loving creation and providence for her and for the whole universe. The hope is that she
will come to the heartfelt knowledge that she has a part to play
in God's one action, which is this universe, and will desire to
know what that part is.

No matter how well one tries to screen people prior to
beginning the full Exercises, some people begin them without a
deep trust in God. In such cases this time on the affective
Principle and Foundation can take a number of days. One Jesuit
tertian spent about ten days struggling with whether he could
entrust his life to the God who had, seemingly, let him down
early in his life. It was time well spent; indeed, the lack of trust
might not have come to consciousness if he had not been mak-

ing the full Exercises with a director. Without this foundation, however, it makes no sense to try to move the retreatant to the next stage of the Exercises. The Exercises are an ordered progression in which one stage depends on the relatively "successful" completion of the prior stage. The whole edifice depends on the solidity of the foundation.[9] If the foundation is not firmly established prior to the beginning of the full Exercises, then the wise director has no alternative but to help the retreatant to allow God to build it firmly.

I hope that it is already apparent that the kind of direction I do and encourage in others requires the ability to listen to the experience of the directee and to adapt one's approach accordingly. The director, in other words, must have developed some of the basic listening skills of the skilled counselor, such as the ability to help the directee to be concrete and somewhat detailed about experience, the ability to respond to the directee with accurate empathy, the ability to ask questions for clarification in a way that does not imply a negative judgment on the directee's experience.[10] Very often directors need much help and supervision to overcome their tendency to want to give answers or to help the person to discern before the actual experience of the directee is sufficiently explored. Before discernment is possible directees must become sufficiently aware of their experiences. Directors who too quickly presume that they know what their directees have experienced run the risk of not permitting "the Creator to deal directly with the creature, and the creature directly with his Creator and Lord" (n. 15) and thus of leading them astray. Later in the chapter I will return to the topic of supervision.

The "First Week"

Retreatants who have a profound experience of the affective Principle and Foundation recognize that God is creating this universe so that all men and women might live in harmony with the Trinity and in community with one another. They also realize that each person has a role to play in God's loving intention for this universe. Such retreatants will want to live out God's plan, but they also know that the world and they themselves are not in harmony with God's plan. Such felt knowledge leads into the First Week of the *Spiritual Exercises* where the desire is to know how both the world and oneself have fallen short of what God intends. At the same time these retreatants want to know that God has not given up on them or on the world. One can put the desire this way: "I want God to reveal to me how God sees me and my world?"

The novelist Brian Moore has captured well this desire at the end of his novel *Blackrobe.* The novel is set in Canada at the time of the French conquest of the native Americans, and poignantly describes the clash of alien cultures as the French Jesuit priests try to convert the Iroquois and Hurons. The protagonist Père Laforgue has witnessed this tragic clash, has himself been tortured by the Iroquois, and has at times doubted the existence of God. At the end of the novel he is baptizing people of the Huron tribe knowing that their baptism will mean the end of their civilization. The novel thus depicts both personal and cultural brokenness and sinfulness. It ends with these words: "And a prayer came to him, a true prayer at last. 'Spare them. Spare them, O Lord. Do you love us?' 'Yes.'" That prayer of Père Laforgue expresses the desire of the retreatant who enters the dynamic of the First Week of the *Spiritual Exercises.*

In the course of the First Week I try to help retreatants to look not only at their own sinfulness and sinful tendencies but also at the history of sin in the world. The first meditation on Triple Sin can be given as in the book of the Exercises, but retreatants can also meditate on the condition of the world at present and then reflect on the historical conditions that have contributed to the present conditions. The headlines of the day's newspapers often can supply the opening for such reflection. The seemingly intractable evils of our day portrayed in the newspapers bring home the power of evil and of the Evil One and show how far from the intention of God our world has strayed. I also suggest that retreatants ask God to reveal their own complicity in this history of sin and evil in the world in a period of prayer that complements the earlier period when they asked God to reveal their salvation history.

During this First Week I also propose scripture texts that help them to face God and Jesus as the sinners they are. Examples are the woman caught in adultery (Jn 8: 1–11), Isaiah 43: 1–7 (given the context that the Israelites are in exile because of their sins), the washing of the feet (Jn 13: 1–11), and Peter's triple profession of love (Jn 21: 15–19). During this time I suggest that they end their prayer periods by looking at Jesus on the cross and speaking directly to him. It is quite difficult for many people who are aware of their sinfulness to look directly into the eyes of Jesus on the cross, but when they do, they come to a deep realization of his love and forgiveness. During this time also they pray the "triple colloquy" suggested by Ignatius, first asking Mary to intercede with Jesus, then asking Jesus to intercede with his Father, and finally begging the Father for that deep knowledge of their own sins and sinful tendencies and also of the disorder of the world in which they live and move and have their being (n. 63). This triple intercession indicates the depth of the desire for freedom from all sins and sinful tendencies and all inordinate attachments.

In directing this week of the Exercises I have assumed that only God can reveal our sins and sinful tendencies to us. Sin is precisely a blind spot which keeps us from knowing ourselves as we really are. So we beg God for God's view of ourselves and our world so that we can repent and try to live out God's dream for us and our world in cooperation with God's grace. Actually, in each of the weeks of the Exercises the *id quod volo,* the desire, is for a personal revelation of God, as we shall see in more detail in chapter 3. I shall allude to the object of this desire in each of the weeks.

During this week retreatants who have for long harbored the deep-seated fear that some secret sins or sinful tendencies, or something of which they are ashamed, could not bear the light of day, somehow would not be forgiven by God, can find themselves freed from an overwhelming burden. Let one example suffice for many. Suppose someone has for years feared that he is a homosexual. With his rational mind he can tell himself that God loves him no matter what his erotic attractions may be, but he cannot admit to God exactly what these attractions are because he fears that God will repudiate him. As long as these fears keep him from being open with God, his prayer experiences will be somewhat superficial. God will seem distant. The director will notice that his description of prayer seems dry and intellectual. There will not be much movement, the kind of movement Ignatius expects during the Exercises. The alert director can help the directee by questioning him about his desires and about how he feels about the way the prayer periods are going. If they have established a good working relationship, the director can point out that his prayer seems dry and overly rational. By judicious questioning and gentle confrontation the director can help the directee to recognize that something is keeping him from closeness to God. In the course of further prayer he may realize what that something is. During this week he has a chance to pour out to God and to Jesus not only his fears but also the content of his fantasies and to discover that God still looks on him with love and care. This experience can disabuse him of the illusion that God's love is conditional, and can lead to the freedom from self-absorption that makes entrance into the Second Week of the *Spiritual Exercises* possible and desirable.

I also hope that retreatants will, during this Week, realize that God also loves this sinful world with all its sinful and corrupting social structures. In other words, during this period in the Exercises retreatants can come to the deep realization that God wants the world itself to be more of a place where men and women can live out God's dream for them, and that God has not given up on the world, in spite of all the horrors perpetrated in it, in spite of the injustice and poverty, the murders and torture so easily verified by a casual reading of the newspaper head-lines. During this Week of the Exercises retreatants can come to recognize God's revulsion at the social injustice in the world while, at the same time, experiencing God's tremendous love for our world and for our feeble efforts to live out God's dream.

The "Second Week"

I look upon the kingdom meditation as an exercise which evokes the deep-seated desire in us for the fulfillment of God's dream for the world and for someone to whom we can give our whole selves in order to fulfill that dream. The parable of the earthly king is of a piece with the myths of the hero and heroine which have been a part of world literature since its inception. The prophecies of the Jewish scriptures which evoke our hopes in Advent are of this type. The early Christians read these prophecies and then pointed to Jesus as the fulfillment and more than fulfillment of them. In a sense the way a person reacts to these myths indicates whether they have the desire of the Second Week. Let me give an example using Luke 4: 16–21. In this pericope Jesus reads from the prophet Isaiah in the syna-gogue and then says: "Today this scripture has been fulfilled in your hearing." If a retreatant hears the words of Isaiah and focuses on herself as one of those in need of healing or freedom, rather than on the figure of Jesus who has a mission, then per-haps she still is in the dynamic of the First Week; the focus is still on her need for healing and forgiveness. But if she thrills to the program of the prophet and wants to be with Jesus on his mission, then she has the desire of the Second Week, which is that Jesus reveal himself to her in order that she may love him more and follow him more closely. In chapter 5 we shall look more closely at the transition points to the four Weeks.

During the Second Week I begin with the first day proposed by Ignatius. The contemplation of the incarnation with its reference to the Trinity looking down upon the world, brings back to mind both the Principle and Foundation and the First Week, and the contemplation of the nativity with the suggestions for the colloquy looks forward to the passion and cross. After this first day I usually suggest a day spent on the first ten chapters of Mark's gospel. People rarely read a whole gospel in one sitting, and Mark's first ten chapters can be read reflectively in less than one prayer period. During the other prayer periods of the day the retreatants go back to those aspects of Jesus' life and ministry and personality that struck them most forcefully. Then, in the next day or two, I suggest a closer look at scenes from the first three chapters culminating in the call of the Twelve. "He went up the mountain and called to him those whom he wanted, and they came to him. And he appointed twelve, whom he also named apostles, to be with him, and to be sent out to proclaim the message, and to have authority to cast out demons" (3:13–15).

For most retreatants these days lead to the point of whether they want to ask to be chosen to be companions of Jesus as the Twelve were chosen. They are then ready to take a day in which they meditate on the value systems of Satan and of Jesus, Ignatius' Fourth Day. Stripped of the medieval imagery, the meditation on the Two Standards strikes a responsive chord in people. Movies such as Woody Allen's "Crimes and Misdemeanors" depict the progression of temptation. In that movie, for example, an honored doctor comes to the point of hiring a hit man to kill his mistress because she threatens to spill the beans to his wife. Reputation and money are on the line; hence, he takes into his own hands the role of God and pays the hit man to kill. Herod's banquet in Mark 6 also depicts the same progression. Because he will lose face among his guests, Herod finally does something he does not want to do, namely, kill John the Baptist. Here again Ignatius suggests a triple colloquy, praying first to Mary, then to Jesus and finally to the Father (n. 147). This triple prayer underlines the reality that these two value systems square off in battle within the individual heart. If I am to live by the values of Jesus, I absolutely need the grace of God, I need to be put under the value system of Jesus by the Father. The meditation on the Three Classes of Persons finishes this Fourth Day.

For the rest of the Second Week I usually suggest the section of Mark's gospel from 8:22 to the end of chapter 10. This section can be looked at as an *inclusio,* since it begins and ends with a cure of a blind man. Moreover, Bartimaeus, after his cure, "followed" Jesus "on the way," the way that leads to Calvary. In this section Jesus predicts his passion three times, and three times the disciples are blind. Jesus also speaks of the costs of discipleship. During these days retreatants continue to ask to know Jesus in order to love him more and to follow him more closely, continue to pray the triple colloquy of the meditation on the Two Standards.

The issue before retreatants is how Jesus wants them to live out their lives as disciples. I take the "election" as an issue of God's election of the retreatant, not, in the first instance, of the election or choice by the retreatant. This stance is also supported by these words of Leo Bakker:

> ...the exercitant does not stand before a whole row of objects of election among which he must choose those which agree more with God's will; rather, according to Ignatius, the exercitant who wants "more" actually finds himself facing only one alternative: a life in which he only *desires* to take on the likeness of his earthly Lord, or a life in which he may *actually* take on this likeness. Election— the grace of the Second Week— is, therefore, nothing else than the inner knowledge of the Lord in order to love him more and to follow him more closely.[11]

In other words, retreatants face the question: does God want me to live out my life as a disciple of the poor Jesus? If the answer is yes, the concrete details of how to live out this choice can only be worked out in the time after the conclusion of the Exercises.

Of course, at this time of election the retreatant may conclude that God's election or call to follow Christ's poor includes a concrete way of living, e.g., as a religious or as a lay missionary. But the concrete details may not work out. At Manresa, Ignatius himself came to the conclusion that God wanted him to work apostolicly in poverty. He also wrongly concluded that Jerusalem was to be the venue of his apostolate. Life after Manresa eventually taught him the concrete way in which God's election of Ignatius would enflesh itself. Another example is provided by a young man who, during the Exercises, came to a profound knowledge and love of the poor Jesus and a conviction that Jesus was calling him to apostolic work. He also concluded that Jesus was calling him to enter the Jesuits. But the Jesuits, for some reason, did not accept him, and he had to look further to see how to concretize his election. Directors need to be aware of the difference between the election to discipleship and the concrete details of a life of such discipleship which can only be worked out in a world where many factors come into play.

The "Third" and "Fourth Weeks"

The Third Week is ushered in by the arousal of the desire in the retreatant to have Jesus reveal what his passion and death were like. In the First Week the retreatant looked at Jesus on the cross, but the desire then was to know that Jesus still looked on her, the sinner, with love. The focus was more on her own needs. Now the focus is on Jesus and what he is suffering. The desire is for compassion for Jesus. Retreatants who have this desire may be surprised, however, at how difficult it is to stay with Jesus in contemplation of the passion. But it could hardly be otherwise.

All of us shy away from pain, suffering and death. If we find it very difficult to face our own suffering and eventual death, we often find it even more difficult to face the suffering and death of those we love. We do not easily ask our loved ones to tell us what they are suffering, and we put off mentioning to them the reality of their imminent death as long as possible. When retreatants enter the Third Week, these dynamics operate even though the desire to share Christ's sufferings is very strong. Directors need to recognize how deep the resistance is and to help their directees face it without getting discouraged. Nowhere else in the Exercises is it so clear that consolation does not necessarily mean feeling happy and content. I have known people who have suffered deeply during this week as they felt not only what Jesus himself suffered, but also what he still suffers in all the sufferings of the people of our world. Yet painful though it was, they knew that they wanted to stay close to Jesus and found themselves desolate when they pulled away from contemplation of his sufferings.

The Fourth Week arrives with the desire to have Jesus reveal the joy of his resurrected life. Here, too, it may not be easy for the retreatant to stay with the contemplation of the risen Jesus. I believe that one source of resistance here is the hidden hope that with the resurrection the cross and death of Jesus will be seen as only a bad dream. But the risen Jesus carries the marks of his passion on him. The past is not undone. The wisdom of Jesus is hard to accept, namely, that he could only be the risen One he now is through the actual life he led and the death he suffered. "Oh, how foolish you are, and how slow of heart to believe all that the prophets have declared! Was it not necessary that the Messiah should suffer these things and then enter into his glory?" (Lk 24: 25–26). The only way to have the joy of the resurrection is to accept it as a grace on God's terms. Another source of resistance, I believe, is a deep-seated reluctance to surrender ourselves totally to God, to accept the fragility and frailty of all our best efforts and our lives and to leave resurrection and the success of the kingdom to the Father. It is very hard for us to believe in practice that the only way to save our life is to lose it, that the only way to enjoy life is not to cling to it with might and main. Again, retreatants need to be reminded that they desire a grace, not something in their power to bring about.

Often enough in a thirty-day retreat there is not much time left to spend on the Contemplation to Obtain Love about which we will have more to say in chapter 11. I usually point it out and suggest that retreatants might well want to continue with this contemplation after the retreat is over. I explain that it is a contemplation, not a meditation. We are here asking for an intimate knowledge of God's great gifts. In Manresa Ignatius had a number of mystical experiences which he describes in his *Autobiography*. These seem to have been the experiential substratum for the Contemplation. Ignatius hopes that the exercitant will experience God's creative touch, God's desire and efforts to share with us as much of himself as he can. In effect, Ignatius hopes that the exercitant will experience the whole world and every moment in it as sacred, as "charged with the grandeur of God."[12]

Ignatius himself seems to have realized that directors needed to be reminded to let the Creator deal directly with the creature. Both in my own practice and in supervising others I have come to realize that reminders are often not enough. Directors too easily want to help with counsel or theology or directions, especially when their directees are experiencing difficulty. In the actual direction session they reveal that their faith in the reality of God's direct dealings with their directees is rather weak. Moreover, in the intensity of the one-to-one direction personality patterns in themselves and in their directees are activated. Transference and countertransference reactions often occur. These can be expected to be rather strong in a thirty-day retreat when the director and directee meet every day and deal with very intimate experiences. As a result groups of directors with whom I have worked have tried to engage in some kind of supervision. Most often the directors gather regularly for peer supervision in a group. The focus of such supervision is not on the absent party (the retreatant) but on the experience of the director. The director presents her experience of directing some- one, revealing her own reactions and thoughts and feelings. The peer group helps her to examine her experience and to under- stand why she is reacting as she does. Directors are encouraged to present experiences which trouble or concern or surprise them. In this way they can learn something about themselves as directors and also can see in the concrete where they need to ask God's help to become better directors.[13]

Conclusion

In this chapter I have tried to show how I approach the direction of the *Spiritual Exercises.* Ignatius discovered in his own experience that God and he could deal directly with one another and that these dealings had an ordered progression. Perhaps because of my training as a psychologist I tend to see this ordered progression in terms of an ever-deepening relation- ship analogous to the development of an intimate human rela- tionship. Any developing intimate relationship between two humans begins with an initial attraction (the affective Principle and Foundation). As the relationship develops, it will gradually erode the egocentric concerns of each of the parties and shift each to concern and care for the other instead of the self (First Week). Moreover, such a developing relationship, if it continues to develop authentically, will lead the two persons to larger con- cerns than just themselves (Second Week). Finally, any intimate relationship must come to grips with suffering and death (Third Week) in order to enjoy fully life itself (Fourth Week). The human analogy, however, pales before the reality of what hap- pens when the Creator deals directly with the creature and the creature with his or her Creator.

2

"WHAT DO YOU WANT?"
THE ROLE OF DESIRES IN PRAYER

"I know; you're going to ask what I want." "As I was driving up to the retreat house, I thought of your perennial question: "What do you want?' and here's what I came up with." I have often noticed that people who see me for some time for spiritual direction or directed retreats say things like this. It even becomes something of a bit of humorous byplay, as though they want to beat me to the punch. Clearly, one of my favorite questions for directees is the one Jesus put to the two disciples who began to follow him, "What are you looking for?" (Jn 1: 38). If directees pick up on this predilection and start asking themselves the question, then, I believe, a good deal of my work as spiritual director is done. If we know what we want in prayer, we are going to find our way. After a practical belief that God wants an intimate relationship with each one of us and that God is directly encountered in our experience, nothing is more important for the development of our relationship with God, for our prayer, in other words, than knowledge of what we want and of what God wants. In this chapter I want to discuss the role of desires in prayer.

Anyone familiar with the *Spiritual Exercises* knows that among the preludes to every meditation or contemplation is "to ask God our Lord for what I want and desire." In the various stages or weeks of the Exercises Ignatius states what the desire is in each case. For example, in the First Week I "ask for growing and intense sorrow and tears for my sins," and in the Second Week I "ask for an interior knowledge of Our Lord, who became human for me, that I may love him more intensely and follow him more closely." In chapter 3 I will try to show that each of the desires of the Exercises is a desire for some particular revelation by the Lord.

On the face of it it looks as though Ignatius is saying: "Here is what you should desire at each stage of the Spiritual Exercises." One conclusion might be to take a person through the four Weeks and just put before him or her what Ignatius gives as the desire. In fact, this has been the procedure in preached retreats, including the preached thirty-day retreats we older Jesuits and other religious made in novitiate and tertianship. But what happened if, as a matter of fact, I did not really desire to know Jesus more intimately when the Second Week was presented to me? Suppose, for example, I was still too afraid of what he thinks of me. In most instances, I would guess, we just presumed that we had the desire if it was Second Week time. But I would contend that without the real desire we never got very intimate with Jesus. Indeed, I believe that "what we really desire" is diagnostic of the stage of the Exercises we are actually in. To demonstrate this thesis we need to look at the role of desires in any relationship.

If you get a call from someone asking for a meeting, your first question, at least to yourself, is, "What does she or he want?" is it not? In fact, many meetings between people come off badly because the individuals involved have mistaken ideas of what each wants. For example, I want to become your friend, and you believe that I want help with homework; you want to help me, but are not even thinking of a deeper friendship. At the end of the meeting both of us are going to be pretty frustrated unless we talk about our different desires and come to some understanding. Often enough relationships become frustrating because of ambivalent or incompatible desires in one or both parties. For example, I want to get closer to you, but I am also afraid of you. Or I want a friendship with you (a happily married woman), but I also want to have an affair. Every intended encounter with another person is accompanied by a desire or desires. We are not always aware of our desires, but they are present, and they condition our behavior in the encounter.

Now suppose that I want to befriend you, and you do not want my friendship. Will my efforts at befriending you get me or you anywhere? Only to frustration and resentment, probably. But suppose that I persist in trying to do nice things for you. What will happen? You will probably get more and more irritated and thus less and less likely to become my friend. And like many a "do-gooder" whose good deeds are rejected, I may eventually wash my hands of you and call you an ingrate who deserves his fate. Friendship is only possible when the desires are mutual, when you freely desire my friendship and I freely desire yours. Friendship cannot be coerced.

"But," someone may object, "we often do things that we do not want to do. Because of my friendship for you, for example, I will go to a movie I don't like." But what do you want? If it is because of friendship with me that you go to the movie, your deepest desire is to please me or to be with me, is it not? The friendship is more important than the movie. I believe that the centrality of desire for the developing of a relationship cannot be denied.

Now let us look at the importance of desires for the relationship with the Lord. In the first chapter of John's gospel the two disciples of John are intrigued by this Jesus whom John has just pointed out as the lamb of God. So they start following Jesus. When Jesus asks them what they are looking for, they say, "Rabbi, where are you staying?" They do not yet have strong desires, it seems; curiosity seems to be the desire. Jesus does not disdain this desire. "Come and see." Unless we have some attraction toward God, some curiosity or hope or desire, we will not take the time to begin our side of the relationship. If I believe in my heart and feelings that God is an ogre, ready to pounce on any infraction, then I may try to placate God, but I will never want to get close. And God, as it were, does handstands to convince us that God really is benign, that God is, as Jesus asserted, Abba (dear Dad, or, since God has no gender, dear Mom). The profligate wonders of nature, our own creation and life, the words of Old and New Testaments, Jesus himself, loving, caring people in our lives — these are all signs of God's desire that we find God attractive and let God come close. But God cannot, or will not, force us into closeness. We must have some desire to get to know God better. Sebastian Moore affirms that God's creative touch which desires us into being arouses in us a desire for "I know not what," i.e., a desire for the Mystery we call God.[14] This experience (understood as the experience of one's creation and continued creation) can be seen as the affective principle and foundation for the development of one's relationship with God. The desire for "I know not what" is what makes our hearts restless until they rest in God.

Many people need help to recognize that they have such a desire. Because of life's hurts they may not recognize any other desire but to be left alone, or not to be hurt any more. Telling such people that God is love has little or no effect. They may need help to let God know that they are afraid and desire to be less afraid. Indeed, they may need help to voice some of their anger at life's hurts which seem to them to have come from the Author of life. The fact that they have not completely turned away from religion indicates that they may still want something from God, even if only an acknowledgement that God knows what happened to them in life. Like Job some may cry out: "know then that God has put me in the wrong, and closed his net around me. Even when I cry out, "Violence!' I am not answered; I call aloud, but there is no justice" (Job 19: 6–7). Only after Job has poured out his sorrows, it seems, can he say: "For I know that my Redeemer lives, and that at the last he will stand upon the earth" (25). In other words, it may take a great deal of pastoral care and patient spiritual direction for some people to come to the point where they can trust life and the Author of life enough to let into their consciousness the desire for "I know not what."

Job's "friends" tried to derail him from expressing his desires to God. In his misery he wants God to speak to him. Job will not lie and say, as his "friends" insinuate, that he deserves his calamities because of his sins. He will not accept the "just world hypothesis" proposed by his "friends," according to which a person's sufferings must be deserved. No, he knows that he does not deserve the awful fate that has befallen him, and he desires to speak directly to God and to hear God's answer. Often enough we Christians are like the "friends" of Job. To a mother who has just lost her only child we might say, "God knows best," and thus make it difficult for her to voice her outrage at God and her need for God's own answer to this awful loss. Sometimes we feel that we have to defend God against the anger directed at God by suffering people. Yet the anger may be the most authentic way for a person to relate to God and to express a desire to know God's response.

Finally, in chapters 38 through 41 God does answer Job out of the whirlwind. The response may not sound very comforting or apologetic to us, but apparently Job was satisfied, for he said: "I had heard of you by the hearing of the ear, but now my eye sees you; therefore I despise myself, and repent in dust and ashes" (42: 5–6). Moreover, then God speaks to Job's "friends," "My wrath is kindled against you and against your two friends; for you have not spoken of me what is right, as my servant Job has" (7). Whatever else God's speech from the whirlwind means, it certainly does not mean that Job has lost God's friendship by voicing so strongly his desire to have God answer him.

Another biblical instance of an attempt to derail a desire directed toward God comes in the first chapter of the first book of Samuel. Hannah, one of the two wives of Elkanah, is barren and miserable. She wants a son. Her husband, Elkanah, seeing her weeping and fasting, says to her, "Hannah, why do you weep? Why do you not eat? Why is your heart sad? Am I not more to you than ten sons?" (1 Sam 1: 8). In other words, Elkanah wants Hannah to forget her desire and be satisfied with what she has. In the story we do not hear Hannah's reply, but her actions tell us that she was not fobbed off by Elkanah's entreaties. She went to the temple. "She was deeply distressed and prayed to the Lord, and wept bitterly" (10). Indeed, when accused of being drunk by Eli, the priest, she says, "No, my Lord, I am a woman deeply troubled. . . I have been pouring out my soul before the Lord" (15). Hannah knows what she wants and is not afraid to tell God over and over what it is.

Often we tell ourselves or are told to quell our desires, to look at all the good we already have. We can be made to feel guilty and ungrateful for desiring what we want. But if we do suppress our desires without being satisfied that God has heard us, then, in effect, we pull back from honesty with God. The result for our relationship with God often is polite distance or cool civility. Perhaps God cannot or will not grant what we want, but for the sake of the continued development of the relationship we need to keep letting God know our real desires until we are satisfied or have heard or felt some response. In 2 Corinthians Paul says, "a thorn was given me in the flesh, a messenger of Satan to torment me.... Three times I appealed to the Lord about this, that it would leave me, but he said to me, "My grace is sufficient for you, for power is made perfect in weakness'" (2 Cor 12: 7–9). Paul could now stop making known his desire because now he knew God's answer. "So I will boast all the more gladly about my weaknesses, so that the power of Christ may dwell in me. Therefore, I am content with weaknesses, insults, hardships, persecutions, and calamities for the sake of Christ; for whenever I am weak, then I am strong" (9–10).

Convictions such as Paul's come not from theological or spiritual nostrums, but from the experience of growing transparency between a Paul and the Lord. Too often we use the hard-won wisdom of a Paul to shortcircuit a similar transparency in our own relationship with the Lord. A woman may, for example, be experiencing the "dark night of the soul" and not like it at all. Her desire may be for it to be removed. She may be helped by the knowledge that others have experienced the same thing before her and been the better for it, but such knowledge does not have to satisfy her desire to be rid of the "dark night." A short circuit in the relationship might occur if she is told by her spiritual director or tells herself to squelch her desire "because the experience is good for you." What she needs to experience is God's response, not a theorem of spiritual theology. She needs to know (really, not notionally) that God does want this darkness for the good of their relationship. Such real knowledge comes only through mutual transparency.

Most of the healing miracles of the New Testament depend on the desire of the recipient for healing. The example of the blind beggar Bartimaeus (Mk 10: 46–52) stands out, but is not unusual. "When he heard that it was Jesus of Nazareth, he began to shout and to say, 'Jesus, Son of David, have mercy on me!' Many sternly ordered him to be quiet, but he cried out even more loudly, 'Son of David, have mercy on me!'" Obviously Bartimaeus will not be hindered from expressing his desire by any number of voices trying to quiet him.

These "voices" can come from within us as well as from without, by the way. "Jesus won't have time for the likes of me; other people have more important problems; things aren't so bad." These interior voices may be expressing our ambivalence about being healed. Just as Bartimaeus had made a way of life out of his blindness, so too we may have made our own physical or psychological or spiritual limitations a way of life and be afraid of what a future without them might be. One person on a retreat thought that he desired healing from a kind of darkness that seemed to rule his life. But then he heard the Lord ask, "Do you want me to heal you of this?" and he had to admit that he was not sure. Interestingly, he felt that God approved the honesty of his response. The inner voices may also arise from our fear of expressing strong desires for healing only to have them dashed. "Suppose I really want to be healed and I hear the answer Paul got? What a disappointment!"[15] Desires are complex and often contradictory. However, once we have allowed the ambivalence and complexity of our desires to surface we have something else to ask the Lord about.

In the Bartimaeus story Jesus calls him over and asks, "What do you want me to do for you?" Bartimaeus is quite clear and unambivalent, "My teacher, let me see again." "Go," says Jesus, "*your faith* has made you well." I have highlighted Jesus' words. Without the faith of Bartimaeus, apparently, this miracle could not have occurred. The miracle requires a partnership between Jesus' healing power and desire to heal and Bartimaeus' faith and desire to be healed. Indeed, Bartimaeus' faith is his desire in action.

An example may help to illustrate this point. Once I was filled with anger and self-pity about the turn a friendship had taken and thought that I was praying for healing. I was contemplating the story of the two blind men in Matthew 9: 27–30. When Jesus asked them, "Do you believe that I am able to do this?" I knew immediately that I was not ready to give up my self-pity and anger. If I did desire healing, it was with the same "but not yet" desire with which Augustine at one time desired chastity. I did not have the "faith" found in the two blind men and in Bartimaeus, a faith that showed itself in unambivalent desire. Another example that shows how desire is faith in action is provided by the father of the boy with the evil spirit reported in Mark 9: 14–29. Instead of asking directly for a healing the father said to Jesus, "but if you are able to do anything, have pity on us and help us." Because he did not believe in Jesus' power to heal, he could not desire the healing directly. "If you are able! — All things can be done for the one who believes." To which the father replied, "I believe; help my unbelief." In effect the man is saying, "Help me to desire healing."

This last example brings us close to the nub of why desires

are the raw material out of which relationships are made. In order for the healing to occur there must be a meshing of desires. Bartimaeus' desire for healing meets Jesus' desire to heal; without both desires there is no relationship, at least no mutual relationship. This point is beautifully illustrated in the story of the leper. "A leper came to him begging him, and kneeling he said, 'If you choose, you can make me clean.' Moved with pity, Jesus stretched out his hand and touched him, and said to him, 'I do choose. Be made clean!' Immediately the leprosy left him, and he was made clean" (Mk 1: 40–42). Clearly desire meets desire. The kind of relationship Jesus desires is a mutual one, where desire meets desire.

The need for a partnership of desires becomes even clearer when we look at friendship. In John 15: 15 Jesus says, "I have called you friends." He then goes on to indicate what that means as far as he is concerned: "because I have made known to you everything that I heard from my Father." From his side the desire has been to be fully transparent, to communicate to them all that he is. His desire meets their desire to know him as fully as possible. Of course, full mutuality of friendship means that they desire to be fully transparent before him and that he desires to know them fully. Take away one side of these desires, and there no longer is a mutual relationship.

On the apostles' part (and on ours) the mere desire for mutual transparency does not carry it off. "Between the cup and the lip...." Our desires are ambivalent and complex; we are also fearful, and our fears get in the way of what we most deeply want. We need help and healing to grow toward mutual transparency with the Lord. But that help is available if we want it. If we notice, for example, that we want to know Jesus better, but are afraid of the consequences, we can ask Jesus for help to overcome our fears. But again we notice that desire is the key to developing the relationship.

The retreatant mentioned earlier who told God that he was not sure that he wanted healing of the darkness that ruled his life provides another example of the reciprocity of relationships. Later in the same day he became more sure that he wanted healing and asked the Lord to heal him. The Lord's response was perplexing; "I can't," he seemed to say. The retreatant was enraged at such a response when his own reluctance had been overcome, and he let God know in no uncertain terms. Yet still later in the day, out of the blue, as it were, he heard the Lord say, "But we can." He knew immediately that the Lord meant that he could live more out of joy than sadness if he kept desiring the Lord's helpful presence rather than withdrawing into himself. "We can" meant partnership.

At the beginning of this chapter I stated that the real desires a person has are diagnostic of where the person is in terms of the four Weeks of the Exercises. Let me now return to that point. If retreatants do not have a real trust in God's loving care and providence, they will not desire that God reveal to them their sinfulness. Without an experienced-based belief in God's goodness and love, without, in other words, what I have called earlier an affective Principle and Foundation, people are too frightened of God to be able to say and mean the last words of Psalm 139: "Search me, O God, and know my heart; test me and know my thoughts. See if there is any wicked way in me, and lead me in the way everlasting" (23–24). If there is no such real desire, then the first Week of the Exercises is not on. And, it seems, at this point God's desire is not so much to reveal sinfulness as to convince the person that God is "Abba." Similarly, if a retreatant voices the desire to know Jesus in order to love him more and to follow him more closely, yet in his prayer continually identifies with those who need healing, perhaps his real desire is to be healed. The desire to know Jesus of the Second Week shows itself in an interest in Jesus himself, his values, his emotions, his dreams, his apostolate. If the retreatant is not really interested in these matters, but *continually* focuses on his own needs and weaknesses, then the Second Week is not really in progress. Jesus, himself, may at this time desire more to heal than to call to companionship. The difference between the first and third week also comes down to a difference in desire. In the first week I desire to know that Jesus forgives *me* (and us), that he died for *my* (and our) sins; the focus is on desiring to have a deep experience of how much Jesus loved us even though he knew how sinful we were. The desire of the Third Week is more to share the passion with Jesus insofar as this is possible. The focus is on what Jesus felt and suffered, and the desire is that he reveal that to me. Retreat directors, I believe, do their most important work when they help their directees to discover what they do in reality want. And so every retreat could begin with a contemplation of Jesus as he turns and says, "What are you looking for? What do you want?" As retreatants hear these words and let them penetrate their hearts, they will come to know better what they desire; in other words, they will know better who they are at this time in their relationship with the Lord.

3

DESIRE FOR GOD'S REVELATION

In this chapter I want to demonstrate that the desires of people who make the *Spiritual Exercises* are for God's personal revelation to them. People sometimes come to retreat with rather vaguely thought-out hopes and desires: "I want to get back to prayer;" "I need to recharge the spiritual batteries;" "I want to pray about a decision I have to make;" "I just want to be alone with God for a while." When directors probe a bit into these desires, they regularly find that retreatants want to experience the closeness and care of God, but hold little hope that God will actually be a felt presence. In other words, some retreatants expect too little of God, have an image of God as being more niggardly with favors than God has revealed of Godself. This image of God may stem from a sense that God cannot be bothered with the "likes of me." It may stem from a sense that God is a distant and almighty figure. With such an image, whatever the source, retreatants will not have those great desires that Ignatius hopes for in the exercitant. They will not be able to enter upon the exercises "with great spirit and generosity toward their Creator and Lord" as the Fifth Introductory Explanation puts it (n. 5). Such retreatants need a different picture of God. However, a new view of God is not attained from theological lectures or homiletic exhortations as much as from a different experience of God. Thus, a retreatant with such an image of God is helped if she is guided to ask God for what she wants and needs, namely, an experience of God that will enable her to expect great things of God.

An example may help. A forty-year-old priest began a thirty-day retreat with a good deal of apprehension. He wanted to rekindle his devotion. But the prospect of praying four to five hours a day for thirty days was not a little daunting. The idea that God would speak intimately to him seemed foreign to him. He expected to "grunt his way through life" with God at a distance. At the same time part of him wanted intimacy with God. In the first few days he was surprised that the contemplation of natural beauty came easy to him and that the days did not drag. But he still could not believe that God would speak intimately with him. He did ask God to help him to believe this. About the fourth day he was "surprised by joy," as it were. He had had an up-and-down day of prayer. When he woke up in the morning, he got into a conversation with God and felt that God was saying: "You are precious in my eyes." In the following few days he seesawed between believing in the experience and the possibilities it evoked and still doubting its validity. Finally about the eighth day the reality of the experience, and of other like experiences, sank in. Here was an experience of God he had secretly hoped for, but also did not expect. From then on he had great hopes and a great desire for God, only occasionally dampened by a return of his old image of self-in-relation-to-God. His image of God— and correlatively of himself— was changed by this prolonged experience.

A retreatant may be a "house divided" as she begins the retreat. She may desire closeness to God, but she may also be afraid of God. She may fear that God will be terribly demanding. She may fear that God will come close as a condemning judge who frowns on her actions. A retreatant like this needs help to put her ambivalent self before God. What she wants and needs is an experience of God that will overcome her fears. She might be encouraged to begin her periods of prayer by asking God to reveal Godself in a way that will not frighten her away. Then she can do something that will give God a chance to respond to her desire. She may take a walk in a park or along the shore; she may quietly read Psalm 139. She wants a revelation of God that will help her to overcome her ambivalence.

Retreatants may also be helped to know God better by knowing how God has been present in their lives up to the present, as we mentioned in chapter 1. Retreatants desire that God reveal to them their salvation history, namely, their history with God. The retreatant asks God to reveal in detail how God has been present throughout the retreatant's life. Then he or she recalls some place or person or incident from childhood and allows the memories to come freely. The idea is to try not to control the thoughts and images and memories, but to trust the process and the Spirit who dwells in our hearts to bring to mind what God wants to reveal at the present time. Some retreatants fruitfully spend many days in such prayer and come to a new and different image of themselves in relation to God, i.e., to a new revelation of God in relation to themselves.

Naturally enough, not every thought, memory, or image is equally important or a revelation of who God has been for the person. But it is extraordinary how fruitful such prayer time is. It often allows the retreatant to "own" here and now reactions, attitudes, and feelings locked in the past. For instance, a retreatant may cry for the first time for his father who died years before and realize that one of the blocks to intimacy with God was his inability to acknowledge his feelings of loss and anger. Most people finish a day or two of such prayer able to say, sometimes for the first time with conviction, the words of Psalm 139: "For it is you who formed my inward parts; you knit me together in my mother's womb. I praise you, for I am fearfully and wonderfully made" (13–14).

Once again we recognize that the desire of the retreatant is for a personal revelation of God, a revelation which will also disclose to the retreatant who he or she is before God. When such desires are answered, then the retreatant "knows" (in the Johannine sense which combines faith, knowledge and love) that God is *his* or *her* God and that he or she is God's son or daughter. The retreatant can affirm with inner conviction the Principle and Foundation of Ignatius.

The Revelation of Sinfulness

Once retreatants have had a rather deep experience of God's personal love and concern for them and have acknowledged the centrality of God in their lives and hearts, they often begin to think of examining their consciences. They become aware of how they have fallen short of God's hopes for them and for the relation with them. The director needs to help them to recognize their desires and to discern where they come from.

We have become so used to seeing the examination of conscience as a thorough self-scrutiny that we can forget the theological truism that only God can reveal sin to us. The sinner, precisely as sinner, is blind to his or her state. The conviction of sinfulness is a gift of God, an act of God's love. Thus, when the desire to examine sinfulness arises, it is important for the director to take time with the retreatant to clarify where the desire comes from. Examination of sins can become an exercise in self-absorption. It may even be a way of resisting the light of God's love and God's view of one's sinfulness. The clearest example of such resistance is the self-scrutiny of the scrupulous person. What such self-scrutiny effectively blocks out (albeit without conscious awareness of such intent) is God's revelation of God as lover and of the scrupulous person's real sinfulness, namely the unwillingness or inability to accept that love. Concern for "my sins" may effectively keep the light of God's scrutiny from illuminating the need for conversion.

If retreatants have come to a deep trust of God's love and concern, they may spontaneously ask God to reveal any wayward ways, or they may be encouraged to do so by the director. They make their own the words of Psalm 139 already quoted: "Search me, O God, and know my heart; test me and know my thoughts. See if there is any wicked way in me, and lead me in the way everlasting" (23–24). God is being asked to reveal God's ways, to root out all that hinders intimacy and discipleship. When the prayer begins this way, the retreatant often is surprised to find that "sins" expected to be on the docket are not even brought to mind. But something else is revealed and becomes the focal point for conversion; for example, an attitude of self-righteousness or an unwillingness to receive. God has been allowed to reveal God's own view of the relationship, and that view turns out to be different than expected. Retreatants often discover that their sinfulness is not so much in their acts of commission or omission as in their unwillingness to be open and honest with God about these acts. They find out that God wants intimacy with them, warts and all, and that they have been preventing that intimacy by being unwilling or unable to speak the whole truth to God. Their sin, in other words, consists, at least partly, in not believing that God would forgive them, that God does indeed love sinners. They also find out that their unwillingness to be open with God stems from their reluctance to look honestly at their lives in God's presence. The revelation of sinfulness reveals who we are, but it also reveals who God is and wants to be for us.

Even when retreatants have experienced the forgiving love of God, they may have difficulty facing in its stark reality the fact that Jesus died for them. That he died for all human beings is accepted and affirmed, but the sticking point comes when one faces the very personal experience that "he died for *me* in the full knowledge of who I am." Retreatants want to believe this truth, but they can also be afraid, sometimes even terrified, of approaching in imagination Jesus crucified and looking him in the eyes. Whatever the source of these fears—whether they arise from the reluctance to accept such love, from the apprehension that Jesus will not be looking at *me* with love or from the fear of the demands such love will make—the fears are real enough, and the prayer can be very difficult. The director does best not to argue with retreatants, but to help them to ask Jesus to reveal himself in such a way that they can accept such love. They are encouraged to share with him their fears and to approach him as best they can. It may take days, but they should not be moved on, because this point is crucial for their subsequent relationship to God and to Jesus. If this stumbling block is removed by the grace of God, then they will experience at a profound level the free and freeing love of God for them precisely as who they are. They will know that they are loved sinners, and they will also know that God really is a lover of sinners.

The Desire to Know Jesus

The desire of the Second Week, "to ask for an interior knowledge of Our Lord, who became human for me, that I may love him more intensely and follow him more closely," is obviously a desire for revelation. One can only know Jesus intimately if he reveals himself. One asks for this grace and then contemplates the gospel stories, not in order to understand the gospels better, but because the gospels are privileged writings to contemplate in order to give the living Lord Jesus a chance to reveal himself. I want Jesus to reveal to me his values, his loves and hates, his dreams and hopes, and especially his hopes for our relationship and for my life. As Jesus takes on more and more reality for retreatants, they may find him more challenging and daunting than they had expected. He may show himself as having desires for them which they resist. He may desire that they give up everything and follow him in apostolic discipleship. They may recognize that they can freely respond "yes" or "no" and that they will not jeopardize his love for them by saying "no." They, too, develop new or different desires toward him; they may desire to be chosen for apostolic discipleship realizing that Jesus is free to choose them or not. The experience of many retreatants in this Week, in other words, is that they are developing an adult relationship to the living Lord Jesus.

A desire for a more intimate revelation of Jesus is the way

many retreatants express the grace of the Third Week. They have come to a personal knowledge and a deep love of Jesus, and now they ask that he share with them his suffering self, that he let them into that suffering and death that made him who he now is. It is important for directors to point out that they are asking for a grace, something that is not in their own power to attain. Many think that they can easily enter the contemplation of the passion and death of Jesus, only to find that their prayer is dry and difficult. One cannot enter into another's sufferings unless the other reveals himself. So retreatants need to ask Jesus to reveal himself so that they can be sorrowful and compassionate with him. When he begins to reveal himself, they may well find that they have asked for more than they expected, and they resist strongly letting this revelation penetrate to their hearts. The Third Week very often is a struggle.

The desire that Jesus reveal his triumph, his joy, the experience of having come through to resurrection so that one can rejoice and exult with him is the grace of the Fourth Week. Here again the director stresses that a grace or a revelation is being asked for. The Fourth Week experience is not automatic, the climax that can be experienced just by contemplating the resurrection narratives. Jesus must reveal himself. Moreover, the retreatant may well resist this self-revelation of Jesus just as he has resisted earlier self-revelations. Resurrection, for example, does not mean sweet revenge on one's enemies. The triumph may not be as one had expected. Once again we find that the desire for revelation is an ambivalent one because God and God's Son are surprising mystery.

Conclusion

When directors and retreatants look at the graces asked for in retreat as a request for revelation, perspectives change. For one thing, people realize more clearly that prayer is a matter of relationship. Intimacy is the basic issue, not resolutions "to be bctter" or answers to problems. Many of life's problems and challenges have no answers; one can only live with and through them. Problems and challenges, however, can be faced and lived through with more peace and resilience if people know that they are not alone. A man's wife will not return from the dead, but the pain is more bearable when he has poured out his sorrow, his anger, his despair to God and has experienced God's intimate presence to him. Secondly, retreatants recognize more clearly that willpower alone cannot achieve "success" in prayer. It is much clearer that what one desires is a gift which only the Other can supply.

Freedom is at the heart of the process. No one can coerce personal revelation or intimacy. God cannot be forced, but neither can the retreatant. There are some graces that God has freely decided to give everyone, if they will accept them. God wants to save and liberate all of us; God loves us all to the point of letting Jesus die for us, and God wants us to accept that love. But the call to apostolic discipleship has not been promised to anyone who asks for it. It may also be that there are certain desires we have, such as to be let into the suffering heart of Jesus, that are not granted or only granted after a long time of waiting. On the other hand, we need to recognize much more clearly that freedom also means that we are free before God. Directors should not try to coerce retreatants to ask for what they do not (yet) want or are too ambivalent to desire honestly. God does not seem to want dumb submission. God wants spontaneous love.

The relationship to God and to Jesus tends to take on a more adult flavor when people begin to look on prayer in this interpersonal way. They realize that they are not asking for graces, much as a child asks for candy, but for intimacy. While they wisely approach such an enterprise with fear and trembling, they nonetheless can do so as adults who know that intimacy requires maturity on their part.

4

THE PRINCIPLE AND FOUNDATION

Many of us have been accustomed to view the Principle and Foundation as a rather dry theological statement of the reality of the human situation. We often fail to recognize that this set of truths is based not so much on deductions from theological premises as on reflection on lived experience in the light of theology. In his monograph in *Studies in the Spirituality of Jesuits*[16] Joseph Tetlow shows convincingly that Ignatius' text is based on experience, the experience of our continuing creation. He maintains that this experience is "that we are being created momently by our God and Lord in all concrete particulars and that we are listening to God's summons into life when we let ourselves hear our most authentic desires, which rise out of God's passionate, creative love for us."[17] Since Ignatius' text and Tetlow's interpretation express a universal, everyone must be able to have an experience that draws him/her to the knowledge, love and service of God. Can we point to an experience that seems universal and which thus could ground these statements?[18]

In *Let This Mind Be In You*, Sebastian Moore suggests that we all have experiences of desiring "I know not what," experiences which are also accompanied by a feeling of great well-being. These experiences, he says, are experiences of being touched by the creative desire of God who desires us into being and continues us in being. "God could," he says, "be defined— or rather pointed to—by this experience, as that which...causes in us that desire for we know not what which is the foundational religious experience."[19] He refers to the autobiography of C. S. Lewis where Lewis describes such an experience:

As I stood before a flowering currant bush on a sum-
mer day there suddenly arose in me without warning,
and as if from a depth not of years but of centuries,
the memory of that earlier morning at the Old House
when my brother had brought his toy garden into the
nursery. It is difficult to find words strong enough for
the sensation which came over me; Milton's "enormous bliss" of Eden...comes somewhere near it. It
was a sensation, of course, of desire; but desire for
what? not, certainly, for a biscuit tin filled with moss,
nor even (though that came into it) for my own
past...and before I knew what I desired, the desire
itself was gone, the whole glimpse withdrawn, the
world turned commonplace again, or only stirred by a
longing for the longing that had just ceased. It had
taken only a moment of time; and in a certain sense
everything else that had ever happened to me was
insignificant in comparison.[20]

Only later in life did Lewis discover that what he desired was
the Mystery we call God.

In *Sacred Journey* Frederick Buechner provides a wonderful example from his own life, an example which also illustrates
how multidimensional such experiences are. After his father's
tragic suicide his mother took him and his brother to Bermuda.
Near the end of his stay he was sitting on a wall watching ferries
come and go with a girl who was also thirteen. Quite innocently,
he says,

our bare knees happened to touch for a moment, and
in that moment I was filled with such a sweet panic
and anguish for I had no idea what that I knew my
life could never be complete until I found it....It was
the upward-reaching and fathomlessly hungering,
heart-breaking love for the beauty of the world at its

most beautiful, and, beyond that, for that beauty east
of the sun and west of the moon which is past the
reach of all but our most desperate desiring and is
finally the beauty of Beauty itself, of Being itself and
what lies at the heart of Being.[21]

Buechner himself acknowledges that there are many ways
of explaining this experience. However, he goes on to say that

looking back at those distant years I choose not to
deny, either, the compelling sense of an unseen giver
and a series of hidden gifts as not only another part of
their reality, but the deepest part of all.[22]

The novel *Dinner at the Homesick Restaurant* provides an
example of an ordinary person. Pearl Tull is an old, blind, dying
woman who was abandoned by her husband and brought up
three children alone. She lives with one of her sons, Ezra, and
his task each day is to read to her some of her diary from childhood. Most of the entries are pretty banal, and Pearl quickly has
him move on. Then comes the final scene before her death. Ezra
riffles through some entries and begins to read:

"Early this morning," he read to his mother, "I went
out behind the house to weed. Was kneeling in the dirt
by the stable with my pinafore a mess and perspiration
rolling down my back, wiped my face on my sleeve,
reached for the trowel, and all at once thought, Why I
believe that at just this moment I am absolutely
happy."
His mother stopped rocking and grew still.
"The Bedloe girl's piano scales were floating out
her window," he read, "and a bottle fly was buzzing in
the grass, and I saw that I was kneeling on such a
beautiful green little planet. I don't care what else

might come about, I have had this moment. It belongs to me."

That was the end of the entry. He fell silent.

"Thank you, Ezra," his mother said. "There's no need to read any more."[23]

Obviously Pearl wanted to remember that foundational experience once more before she died; perhaps, too, she wanted Ezra to know that she had had that experience.

Not everyone who has such experiences interprets them as experiences of God as Frederick Buechner did. C. S. Lewis, for example, did not do so until much later in life. But a believer can do so and can also draw out their implications. Notice that the experiences speak of desire, desire for "I know not what." In another book Lewis describes the Joy he experienced as "an intense longing" which, though intense and even painful, is somehow a delight, indeed a greater delight than the fulfillment of any another desire.[24] Moreover the experience includes a sense of great well-being. While in the experience we do not worry about ourselves, our worth, our goodness. We seem to take for granted our being in the world. Moore interprets the experience, quite rightly, as an experience of being desired into existence by God. Hence, we are desirable.

However, let us not miss the most significant aspect of these experiences. The experiences happen in the present, not at the moment of creation in the past. Our image of the creation of the universe refers to something that happened in the distant past, at the moment of the big bang. When we imagine God creating us, we tend to think of our creation as happening when we were conceived or born. But the experiences we have been discussing are described as happening to people already alive. If these are experiences of the creative touch of God, then we are talking of an action of God that is going on continually, not of an action that happened in some distant point in time. When we have such experiences, we are experiencing the present action of God.

How are we to understand such an assertion? The late Scottish philosopher John Macmurray developed a philosophy of the person based on the primacy of action over thought.[25] Action includes thought, since any action is intended. When I act, I know what I intend to do. Events are different from actions in that events are not intended; they happen. Actions include events. Let me give an example of an action as Macmurray understands the term. This book is one action of mine since it is governed by one intention. I want to present my approach to the Exercises in such a way that it will have an influence on you, the readers. This one action includes many other actions, e.g., the many actions of rewriting it, and many events, e.g., the typing skills that occur without my intention. My one action, since my intention is to have an influence on you, also depends on my audience and their willingness to pay attention to the book. Thus the printed book in your hands and before your eyes is my one action. In reading and reflecting on this book you are also encountering me. In an analogous way we can understand the universe as one action of God. Hence, God is always active, always doing his thing, as it were. Thus, at every moment of existence of the universe God is creating this world and everything in it, and we are encountering God whether we are aware of it or not.

If the universe is one action of God, then God has one intention in creating it. What does God intend with this one action which is the universe? We only know the intentions of persons (and only persons can perform actions) if they reveal them to us. If you do not reveal to me the intention of your action in my regard, I may infer that you intended to help me, but I may be wrong. You may have just acted inadvertently. I can only *know* your intention if you reveal it to me truthfully. If this is true of human beings, how much more true is it of God! Has God revealed to us his intention in creating the universe? Christians believe that God has done so in the person of Jesus the Christ.

The kingdom of God which Jesus preached can be seen as the intention of God in creating the universe. God, it seems, creates this universe to invite all persons to enter the community life of the Trinity. Moreover, this intention has implications for our present age; the kingdom of God is both of this world and not of this world. God wants all persons to live as sisters and brothers of Jesus and in harmony with the whole created universe. Hence, God has a stake in how each of us lives our lives. Tetlow, in his monograph, speaks not so much of the kingdom of God as of "God's project" which seems to come down to the same thing. God's project

> suggests...a finite reality that exists in God but that is not God. A project is a concrete event, an ongoing activity that requires improvisation and adjustment... To God's project, all things great and small are required to make a contribution out of the self, and indeed will make a contribution whether by choice or not, whether embracing God's hopes or attempting to frustrate them.[26]

Thus, when we have foundational experiences such as I described earlier, we are experiencing the creative action of God, which is always at work to bring us and all persons under the reign or kingdom of God, into the community life of the Trinity. We may not draw out all the implications of such experiences but, nonetheless, I believe, we can do so. In fact, Ignatius has drawn out these implications from his own experiences and distilled them, albeit in a language colored by his own age and theology, in the Principle and Foundation. This is the point of Tetlow's monograph. When we experience the desire for "I know not what," we are experiencing God's one creative action which calls each one of us and the whole universe into being with the intention of drawing all persons into the one community which is the Trinity. No wonder C. S. Lewis could say that he was "surprised by Joy," by a desire that "had taken only a moment of time" but which made "everything else that had ever happened to me…insignificant in comparison."

When I have the experience of desiring "I know not what," I am experiencing God creating me *now* in all the particulars of my present existence. While in thrall to that experience I do not worry about my past failures and sins or about what the future might hold. I feel at one with the universe and as whole as I could possibly be. Moreover the desire I experience is the deepest desire within me. That desire is in tune with God's one intention in creating the universe, and that desire can become the ruling passion of my life, if I let it. When we experience this desire, it is God's Holy Spirit drawing us into the community which is the Trinity. While we are in the power of this desire, everything else becomes relative before the absolute Mystery we desire. Moreover, insofar as this desire reigns in our hearts, we desire to live out our lives in harmony with this desire and want to do whatever will more readily bring us to the object of our desire. Hence, we want to live in harmony with God's creative purpose in creating us, to choose what will be more in tune with our desire for union with God. Ignatius spells out the implications of the foundational experience of God's creative touch in the Principle and Foundation.

Because God is God and because our only ultimate happiness lies in living in harmony with God's intention for the universe and for each one of us, Ignatius calls upon us to be "indifferent" to all created things. In his recent translation Ganss notes that the term is a key technical term in Ignatian spirituality. However, "(i)n no way does it mean unconcerned or unimportant. It implies interior freedom from disordered inclinations."[27] In the monograph already cited Tetlow translates "indifferent" by "at balance." The term "at balance" comes much closer to Ignatius' intent. In the throes of the desire for "I know not what" we do not want anything else to get in the way of the fulfillment of that deepest desire. Thus, before every choice we want to be at balance in order to discern or discover what will more surely bring us what we most deeply desire.

Roger Haight in his enlightening book *Dynamics of Theology* makes the point that "(t)he symbol of the kingdom of God can mediate the experience that as personal and as creator God has a will and intention for creation and that, as a creature, the self participates in that intention."[28] Later he notes the transforming power of this symbol.

> The special note of the kingdom of God is that the one encountered, God, is encountered as having a divine intention for the world and human history. The symbol thus appeals more directly to human will and influences more pointedly human action. An appreciation of its transcendent meaning fairly demands a conversion to a desire to be in conformity with God's will. The symbol thus transforms natural ethics into an expression of God's will. It transforms a person's responses to the world into simultaneous responses to God. It transforms goals and ideals into the goals and ideals of God. It can thus have an impact on the transformation of the world. The kingdom of God is of this world and transcendently more than that.[29]

The experience that underlies the words of the Principle and Foundation leads the person who takes it seriously to want to make the full *Spiritual Exercises* in order to be able to be freed from anything that will hinder the freedom to choose what is more in tune with what God wants and to be able to discern better what that is.

Conclusion

In this chapter we have been reflecting on the Principle and Foundation and on the experiences upon which it is based.

Ignatius' text is not derived from theological premises although theological premises and principles are at work in the elaboration of the written exercise. The experience that underlies it seems to be an experience of God creating this universe and everything in it with the intention of drawing all persons into the community life of the Trinity and into harmonious relations with one another and with the whole universe. Because God is the One Creator, this experience is available to all people according to their capacity. However, even those who have vivid and even awesome experiences of this creative touch of God may not, and often do not want to, pay enough attention to the experiences and to draw out their implications for their lives. For those who do pay attention and who want to draw out the implications of their experience of the Mystery who calls everything and "me" into being for a purpose, Ignatius offers the *Spiritual Exercises* as a powerful means "to overcome oneself, and to order one's life, without reaching a decision through some disordered affection" (21). Because such people experience in an overpowering way what God intends with the universe, with every person and with "me," they recognize the deep disorder of our world and of human beings and of "myself," and they beg God to convert them and all human beings. Moreover, in our day, because we are so aware of the interdependence of everything in the universe, the experience of God's creative action brings us to recognize how contrary to God's intention are the institutions and social structures that influence all our lives, and we beg God to give us the courage and the willingness to do our part to change these unjust institutions and structures. I believe that the Thirty-Second General Congregation of the Society of Jesus was moved by the spirituality of the Principle and Foundation (and of the Contemplation to Attain Love) to the insight that in our modern world work for justice is constitutive of every apostolate that deserves the name Christian.

5

TRANSITION POINTS IN THE DYNAMIC
OF THE EXERCISES

In this chapter I want to look at the transition points in the dynamic of the *Spiritual Exercises*. That is, I want to indicate the kinds of experiences I look for in a retreatant that demonstrate a readiness to begin a particular set of exercises, called "Weeks." The *Spiritual Exercises* are not a drill that one goes through without any regard to what one is experiencing. The director's main task, after listening, is to help the directee to know what he or she authentically desires. These desires can be seen as touchstones for the readiness to move to a new stage of the Exercises.

The Principle and Foundation

As we noted in the last chapter, the Principle and Foundation is the fruit of Ignatius' experience as well as of his later study of theology. Ignatius, after much spiritual agony, came to experience God as the deepest desire of his heart; he realized that he was created for God and that nothing else would satisfy him. Moreover, through his experiences at Manresa, he came to have a felt knowledge of God's architectonic purpose for the creation of the universe. In the Principle and Foundation he tried to distill the fruit of those experiences in the light of his later theological studies.

In effect, Ignatius came to believe, through mystical experience, that the perfect community which is the Trinity, motivated purely by love, creates a universe where persons created in the image of God are continually being drawn by the cords of divine love into the community life of the Trinity. In the depths of our hearts we are being drawn by a desire for union with God and thus with all other persons. Ignatius came to believe that the Trinity wants each of us to live our lives in order to be part of the dream of God, the kingdom of heaven. We cannot, therefore, ultimately be happy and at peace in this life unless our lives are in tune with God's dream for the universe and for each one of us. If we have this experience of God as the Creator who loves us into existence for community with God, then we will have a positive spiritual identity; we will know that we are beloved of God, the apple of God's eye. I have called this experience the affective Principle and Foundation needed to make the *Spiritual Exercises*. With this experience relatively firmly established in our hearts we will, at least inchoatively, realize that we should not let anything get in the way of attaining the end God has in mind for us. We will want to beg God to remove from us all inordinate attachments (which Gerald May[30] calls addictions); hence we will be ready to begin the *Spiritual Exercises*.

I suspect that many of us know from our own and others' experience that it is often difficult to let this experience of God's creative love and dream for us take root in our hearts. A poor self-image can get in the way, as can an image of God as one who, as I mentioned above, is "always snooping around after sinners."[31] Scrupulous people, for example, have the devil's own time coming to believe that God loves them "warts and all." It took four years of careful spiritual direction by Ignatius before Pierre Favre, who later became one of the best directors of the Exercises, was ready to make the *Spiritual Exercises*. Ignatius himself was so plagued by scruples that, he tells us, he came close to suicide.[32] Only after a long time of siege by such scruples did he come to the belief that God was not a tyrant. We will only ask God to purify us of our inordinate attachments and to reveal to us our sins and sinful tendencies when we believe in our bones that God is on our side, that God has our good at heart.

If what I have just noted has any validity, then we need to be patient with ourselves and with those to whom we minister, willing to take the time and to use our ingenuity to help ourselves and others to have, and to have confidence in, such experiences of a loving creative God who invites us into community with the Trinity. These experiences are the firm foundation upon which a developing relationship with God is built.

Before this foundation is firmly built people live in an illusory world. They believe that God needs to be placated, and yet is in a real sense implacable. They try, as Paul did, to fulfill the letter of every law in order to deserve, if not the love of God, at least God's grudging acceptance. The illusion comes down to the belief that "I am rotten to the core and unlovable." Many people live in this illusory world. Those who minister in the church need to develop the spiritual techniques or pastoral practices that will help people to overcome this illusion and to come to a basic trust in God. Only with such a grasp of reality will they (and we) be able to enter the "First Week" of the Exercises which requires the authentic desire of directees to have God reveal to them how they and our world have fallen short of God's dream for them and for the world.

The "First Week"

When people are becoming relatively firmly grounded in the experience of God as a loving Creator, as the Abba of Jesus, they often experience a sort of honeymoon period in prayer. They relish spending time relating to God; prayer seems easy and delightful. But the honeymoon period cannot last forever. We all know that we have fallen short of the glory of God. We become aware of our resistances to further closeness to God. We want God to remove from us everything that hinders further closeness to God, but at the same time we are afraid of what such a removal will entail. We come to recognize that the world is not at all the garden of Eden God intended. God has begun to

reveal to us our own and our society's sins and sinful tendencies. We are entering the dynamic of the First Week of the
Spiritual Exercises where our desire is that God reveal to us our
own and our world's sinfulness, forgive us and enable us to live
more and more in the freedom of the children of God.

As we have seen earlier, the movements of the *Spiritual
Exercises* are driven by desires, the *id quod volo*, of the second
or third prelude Ignatius puts before every meditation or contemplation. These desires cannot be forced; they must be
authentic desires of our hearts. If we do not have the desire
Ignatius expects to drive the dynamic of the First Week, for
example, the only thing we can do is to ask God to give us the
desire. One of the key questions we can put to ourselves for our
own prayer and to those we direct is: "What do I really want
right now from God or in my relationship with God?" Honesty
about our real desires is crucial for growth in our relationship
with God, and indeed, in any relationship. In giving the
Exercises to groups of people we need to keep in mind that the
people in the group will vary widely in their desires. As we give
"points" for prayer, it would be good to remind our listeners to
move with their own authentic desires.

In the First Week of the Exercises, then, my desire is that
God reveal how far I have fallen short of God's dream for me
and how my inordinate attachments (addictions) keep me from
living out God's dream. But I also want to know that God still
loves me, warts and all; I want to know that I am a loved sinner.
Only such knowledge will give me the grace and the impetus to
try to overcome my sinful tendencies. Moreover, I want God to
reveal to me how far my society, my culture, my church, my
world have fallen short of God's dream without losing God's
loving care.

The fact that we need reassurance about God's love of us
sinners indicates that at this stage of our spiritual journey we
also labor under an illusion. It is difficult for us to believe in our
bones that God loves sinners. Yet Jesus died for us *sinners*. This

illusion, like the one which says "I am rotten to the core and totally unlovable," also dies hard. Yet only with its death and burial can we be free. While we live with this illusion, we continually try to prove that we are lovable; we continually try to save ourselves. Only if we can let Jesus wash our feet when he and we know our sinfulness, only if we can look into the eyes of Jesus dying on the cross for our sins and there see love, are we living in the real world which is still, in spite of all its crookedness, a world where God continues to draw us into community with the Trinity, where Jesus gave up his life precisely for us sinners.

When we are freed from this illusion, then we know in the depth of our hearts: "For God so loved the world that he gave his only son, so that everyone who believes in him may not perish but have eternal life. Indeed, God did not send the Son into the world to condemn the world, but in order that the world might be saved through him" (Jn 3: 16–17). With this deep heartfelt knowledge we can speak to Jesus on the cross as a friend speaks to a friend. Then we will be able to ask ourselves without being driven by unhealthy guilt feelings, but by genuine love and shame: "What have I done for Christ? What am I doing for Christ? What ought I to do for Christ?" Now I am, perhaps, ready to allow the desire to know, love and follow Christ rise in my heart.

The "Second Week"

The desire of the Second Week of the Exercises is expressed in the third prelude Ignatius suggests for each contemplation. "Here it will be to ask for an interior knowledge of Our Lord, who became human for me, that I may love him more intensely and follow him more closely" (n. 104). A fundamental shift in orientation has occurred in those who have this desire. Prior to this shift the focus has been on ourselves and our needs. We have wanted to know in a heartfelt way that God is where we are, with us in our brokenness, our sinfulness, our desperate need. With this shift in desire we now want to be where Jesus is; we want to know him and his values and his mission and we want to be part of that mission.[33] The difference might be illustrated by two different images of ourselves in relation to Jesus. In the First Week we are like the blind man Bartimaeus who wants Jesus to give him succor, to heal his blindness. In the Second Week we are like Bartimaeus who, now seeing, follows Jesus "on the way" (Mk 10: 52).

Ignatius did not believe that many people were ready for this kind of shift of perspective. Hence he was slow, it seems, to give the full Exercises. There are many who, because of the physical or psychological traumas suffered in life, find it almost impossible to focus for long on anything but their own need for healing. I realize that I am reading into the text, but I have used the man from whom the legion of demons was driven out as an example. After the legion was driven out, "the man who had been possessed by demons begged him that he might be with him. But Jesus refused, and said to him, 'Go home to your friends, and tell them how much the Lord has done for you, and what mercy he has shown you'" (Mk 5: 18–19). Perhaps, we could say, he was too scarred by what he has suffered to be able to make the radical shift that discipleship with Jesus entails. At any rate, we might keep in mind the possibility that we ourselves or those to whom we minister can only be hurt by being pushed into a desire to follow Jesus which is beyond our capacities.

Those who desire to know Jesus in order to love him more and to follow him more closely will also encounter resistances to the call of Jesus. They will be as blind as the disciples who, after each of the three predictions of the passion, show how completely they have missed the reality of the call. After all, those who follow Jesus too closely may, and indeed will, suffer the same fate as he suffered or at least something similar. Here the source of the resistance is much more realistic. The disciples, when they finally became like Christ, did suffer persecution and martyrdom. Throughout the ages those who have become, through close personal relationship, like Christ have suffered as he suffered. Yet even here an illusion lies behind the resistance. The illusion is that we can control our lives and our fate. If we surrender ourselves to the following of Christ, we fear that we will lose control of our lives and our fate. Yet this fear keeps us from what we most desire at this stage of the spiritual journey, namely closeness to Jesus. Throughout the gospels Jesus contrasts faith and fear, and continually points out how useless fear is. In the final analysis Jesus' call to discipleship faces anyone who hears the call with these words of Jesus:

> If any want to become my followers, let them deny themselves and take up their cross and follow me. For those who want to save their life will lose it, and those who lose their life for my sake, and for the sake of the gospel will save it. For what will it profit them to gain the whole world and forfeit their life? Indeed, what can they give in return for their life? (Mk 8: 34–37)

Ignatius, of course, was astute enough a spiritual guide to know that we cannot follow Jesus in this way without the grace of God. In the meditation on the Two Standards he indicates quite clearly that the two standards or value systems run right through each human heart. Hence, he proposes the triple colloquy in which we ask Mary, then Jesus, then the Father to put us under the standard of Christ. We are addicted to possessions, to our reputations, to our honor, and so we cannot, by ourselves, embrace the values of Christ. Yet these values are the real values that bring true happiness and peace in this life and in the next. In this sense Christianity is what John Macmurray in *Persons in Relation* calls "real religion" in this remarkable statement which I so much enjoy citing:

The maxim of illusory religion runs: "Fear not; trust
in God and He will see that none of the things you
fear will happen to you"; that of real religion, on the
contrary, is "Fear not; the things that you are afraid of
are quite likely to happen to you, but they are nothing
to be afraid of."[34]

Ignatius suggests that those who want to be intimate fol-
lowers of Jesus must beg over and over again to be freed from
their fears and illusory values in order to embrace the values of
Jesus.

The "Third Week"

The desire of the Second Week of the Exercises is "for an
interior knowledge of Our Lord, who became human for me,
that I may love him more intensely and follow him more closely." We want to know his values, his loves, his hates, his
dreams, his hopes. We want to know his heart so that we might
be so much in love with him that nothing, not even our fear of
suffering and of death, will get in the way of following him. As
we are given the grace of this Week, we find ourselves more and
more focused on Jesus, less and less on ourselves. Such a focus
is not an achievement of our own will, but a gift of God for
which we must continually beg. Indeed, the focus is not a once-
and-for-all-time gift for most of us; our self-centeredness dies
hard and may only be finally overcome with the grave. I wonder
whether the experience of how difficult it was for self-centeredness to be overcome led to the theological postulation of the
existence of purgatory.

Nonetheless, those who do have the desire of the Second
Week are gradually freed of enough of their self-centeredness
that they can ask for the graces of the "Two Standards" and of
the "Three Degrees of Humility." Jesus does become the love of
their lives, their closest friend, their dearest companion. As they

come to the end of this stage of their spiritual journey, they—like Bartimaeus after he receives his sight—want to follow Jesus along the way (Mk 10: 52), and the way is the "way of the cross." They are ready to begin the Third Week.

The desire of this Week, as Ignatius articulates it, is: "to ask for sorrow, regret, and confusion, because the Lord is going to His Passion for my sins" (n. 193). Once again it is important to note that Ignatius is talking of a "desire" and that desires are not under our control. To desire to have compassion for Jesus, to suffer with Jesus, is a gift of the love for Jesus that has grown in our hearts throughout the Second Week. Moreover, the presence of the desire does not preclude conflicting desires. Think of how difficult it is for very close friends or loved ones to share pain, suffering and dying. I may want to suffer with my closest friend, but I also fear the consequences of that desire. To share his or her suffering cuts me to the quick. If he or she dies, I lose "half my soul," as Augustine described a dear one; no one easily accepts such a loss. Moreover, my friend may not want to increase my pain by sharing what is really going on in him or her. Those who have worked with the terminally ill note that often both the dying person and her loved ones are terribly lonely precisely because of the mutual fears of "hurting one another," of "making it worse" for one another by sharing their real feelings.

In the case of Jesus we presume that he wants to share his suffering with those who desire to suffer with him; we presume that he wants to give as much of himself to us as we want and can take. (Cf. the Contemplation to Obtain Love, First Point, n. 234.) The ambivalence lies in us. Moreover, we cannot presume that even a relatively deep experience of the Second Week of the Exercises will lead, during this retreat, to a deep desire to suffer with, to have compassion for Jesus. What we can hope for is that during our continuing relationship with Jesus this desire will grow in us as a gift of his love for us. A very deep experience of

the Third Week may only come many years after one has fin-
ished the full *Spiritual Exercises.*

Social psychologists speak of the "just world hypothesis"[35]
which unconsciously guides much of our thoughts, feelings and
behavior. According to this hypothesis suffering is deserved.
Thus, if we hear that someone has cancer of the lungs, we presume that he has been a heavy smoker. If a mud slide wipes out
a whole town, we wonder why the people built their town in that
place. If a woman is raped, there is a tendency for people to presume that she went to the wrong part of town or made a poor
choice of companion or got what she was asking for. We want to
find a reason for a calamity. To understand this dynamic reflect
on your own reactions when you have heard some piece of bad
news regarding yourself. Behind the almost instinctive "Why
me?" lies the "just world hypothesis," and the only answer that
makes sense is that I must have done something wrong. If
calamities are not somehow deserved, then we are all at risk at
any moment, and that is a frightening prospect. This "just world
hypothesis" makes it difficult for anyone of us to enter deeply
into the suffering of another, no matter how close. In the case of
Jesus the "just world hypothesis" is totally exploded. Here the
absolutely innocent one suffers horribly—another reason why it
is difficult for us to desire wholeheartedly to suffer with, to have
compassion for Jesus.

Some of the more bizarre theological theories to explain
the suffering of Jesus might well stem from the unconscious
sway of the "just world hypothesis." For instance, the theory
that Jesus had to suffer so horribly in order to satisfy God's
anger at the sins of humans. Or that only the suffering of a
human being who was God could make up for the infinite indig-
nity suffered by God through sin. These theories, it seems to me,
are concocted to explain why Jesus, the innocent one, had to
suffer so horribly, thus safeguarding the "just world hypothesis."
Yet anyone not beguiled by the hypothesis might ask how such

theories square with Jesus' revelation of God as his "Abba," "Daddy," (or "Mommy") and as overflowing love.

Thus, we must expect that no matter how strong our desire to suffer with Jesus is there will be internal resistances to that desire. Death threatens us with annihilation, with the loss of all the relationships that make us who we are. In his Pulitzer Prize-winning book, *The Denial of Death,* Ernest Becker demonstrated quite well how pervasive in our culture the fear of death is, and how desperately we strive to deny its possibility.[36] All the psychological defenses we put up to deny the reality of death will raise their heads as we approach the Third Week of the *Spiritual Exercises.*

Because of these resistances Ignatius has us beg for what we desire over and over again. He knows firsthand that one experience of compassion for Jesus will not suffice to overcome the resistances. But in spite of the strength of the resistance God's grace is not defeated.

> People do receive this gift of sorrow and compassion for Jesus, and they know that their sorrow is different from the sorrow they experienced in the First Week of the Exercises when they contemplated Jesus on the cross. Then they were sorry for their sins and marveled that in spite of the sins which had put Jesus on the cross he still looked on them with love. Now they are not focused on themselves much at all, but on Jesus and what he has gone through and is going through. One woman came in during a retreat with tears streaming down her face and said, "He's dead; I'm glad that his agony is over." And people who receive this grace of compassion for Jesus find that the compassion spills over to compassion for all the suffering people of this world. Indeed, they sense that Jesus is still suffering in all the people who suffer, especially in those who are oppressed and ground

down as he was. I think that such compassion for a suffering world means taking on the heart of Christ and the compassion of God. God, I believe, is revealing his own reactions to the horrors human beings perpetrate on one another and on God's beloved Jesus. The mystical body of Christ is experienced in a mysterious way when God gives us this gift of compassion for Jesus' suffering and the suffering of untold others.[37]

It may be that the deepest motivation for work for justice in our world arises from the compassion of the Third Week.

The "Fourth Week"

Ignatius expects that in those who have experienced compassion for Jesus in some depth God will elicit a desire "for the grace to be glad and to rejoice intensely because of the great glory and joy of Christ our Lord" (n. 221). This shift in desire ushers in the Fourth Week of the Exercises. Notice that the retreatant asks for a grace, something not in one's own power to achieve. Secondly, notice that we ask to rejoice for Jesus' sake.

The fact that we ask for a grace in this Week indicates that the experience of joy in the resurrection of Jesus does not come automatically. And indeed, we do experience resistance to this grace, which seems strange indeed. However, to experience this intense joy we have to be able to notice the wounds in Jesus' hands and feet. The resurrection is not a return to the *status quo ante*, not an undoing of the horrors of the crucifixion. To experience the joy of Jesus we must be able to accept the mysterious "necessity" of such a horror. "Was it not necessary that the Messiah *should* suffer these things and then enter his glory?" (Lk 24:26). The only way that Jesus could be the glorified Jesus he now is (rather than some other Jesus without the marks of these particular wounds) was the way of the cross. This is the wisdom of Jesus.

It is very hard for us to come to this wisdom. In fact, on our own we cannot come to it. We need the grace of God. Hence, we must beg God to be able to rejoice with Jesus. To rejoice with him we must accept his cruel death. It was not a bad dream, just as the pains and sufferings and losses we suffer and will suffer in life are not bad dreams. I believe that we also cannot fully rejoice in the life of our loved ones who have died and experience their risen life until we can accept their suffering and death. Not only does the fear of death keep us from fully enjoying this life, it also keeps us from rejoicing with the risen Jesus and with our loved ones who have joined him. I want to repeat once again Macmurray's maxim of real religion. "Fear not; the things that you are afraid of are quite likely to happen to you, but they are nothing to be afraid of."[38] The resurrection of Jesus shows real religion at its best. The passion and death really did happen, but, Jesus says, they are nothing to be afraid of. When we receive the grace of rejoicing with Jesus in his glory, then we want to shout Alleluia over and over again.[39]

Conclusion

In this chapter I have tried to show some of the experiences and desires of retreatants that indicate where in the dynamic progression of the *Spiritual Exercises* they are. Obviously progress in the spiritual life is not a matter of smooth progress from one plateau to another. The experience of being a loved sinner is not a once-for-all achievement which never needs to be repeated. The development of any relationship, and especially of the relationship with the Lord, is fraught with many peaks and valleys, with periods of strong development in intimacy and periods of regression to early stages of the relationship. Even a very deep experience of the full *Spiritual Exercises*, even one which culminates in a mystical experience of the Contemplation to Obtain

Love, does not preclude later regressions to early stages in the relationship with the Lord. However, once one has experienced the heights of the relationship, one knows how much God wants to give of Self and thus whets the appetite to desire to return to that depth of relationship.

6

IGNATIAN CONTEMPLATION: THE USE OF IMAGINATION IN PRAYER

What was the original genial insight of Ignatius of Loyola? I would say that it was the idea that God can be found in all things, that every human experience has a religious dimension, has religious meaning. The point is illustrated in the very first chapter of the autobiography Ignatius dictated to Gonçalves da Càmara. Ignatius, the fiery, brave, womanizing, ambitious knight, is convalescing at the castle of Loyola from the shattering of his leg by a cannonball. He tells us that he was much given to imagining himself as a knightly hero winning the favor of a great lady. He would spend hours in such daydreams. Since, however, he could not get the romantic novels he delighted in at the Loyola castle, he began to read the only reading matter at hand, a life of Christ and a book of lives of saints. What he read also fed his imagination, and he began to engage in daydreams of outdoing the saints in austerities in the following of Christ. Again, these daydreams would last for hours. For a long time he did not notice any difference in his reactions to these two sets of daydreams. Yet there was a difference. During the knightly daydreams he felt exhilarated, but after them he felt "dry and unhappy." During the daydreams about imitating the saints, he also felt exhilarated, but after these he "remained happy and joyful." He then says:

> He did not consider nor did he stop to examine this difference until one day his eyes were partially opened and he began to wonder at this difference and

to reflect upon it. From experience he knew that some thoughts left him sad while others made him happy, and little by little he came to perceive the different spirits that were moving him; one coming from the devil, the other coming from God.[40]

I believe that this little story depicts the emergence of the core of Ignatian spirituality, that God can be found in all things. If God can be discovered in daydreams, then God can be found anywhere. In this chapter I want to reflect on the way God used the imagination of Ignatius to lead him to conversion and on how the Ignatian Exercises suggest the use of imagination in prayer.

Obviously Ignatius had a very strong imagination. He loved to read the romantic novels of his time. They fired his imagination to dream of doing great exploits for his king, his country and his "grande dame." He is not alone in this liking for romance, for heroic tales. Think of the popularity of the Western novel and movie in the United States, which enkindled the imaginations of countless people to imagine themselves as the hero or heroine bringing peace and justice to a harsh land. Think of the popularity of J. R. R. Tolkien's trilogy *The Lord of the Rings* in which wizards, elves, dwarfs, human beings and hobbits (halflings) battle together to defeat the Dark Lord who threatens doom to the world. I have read the trilogy five times, and each time tears come to my eyes when Frodo and the other hobbits are praised by the triumphant host for what they have accomplished to help defeat the Dark Lord. Aragorn, the King in the trilogy, is almost the exact image of the king used by Ignatius in his kingdom meditation in the Exercises for he, too, shares all the toils and dangers of his men, leads them through the valley of the dead, and gives his all to save the world from the Dark Lord. Ignatius ate and drank such stories and they fired his ambition and desire to do great things.

But God used this strong imagination to draw Ignatius to

another kind of ambition. The gospel stories and the lives of saints are imaginative literature too. They can fire the imagination, and in Ignatius' case they did. You can imagine his dismay when he discovered these were the only books available in Loyola. Gradually, however, they caught his interest, piqued his imagination, and the very same ambition which drove him to want to do great knightly deeds now took over to let him imagine himself doing the same heroic deeds that the saints did. And in Christ he found a king better than all imagined earthly kings. Finally, he noticed that the two sets of heroic imaginings had different repercussions in his heart. Ignatius discovered that the spirit of God was operative in both sets of imaginings, in the worldly imaginings to help him to taste the ultimate vanity of such exploits, and in the images of following Christ to help him to taste the lasting joy of being with Christ. Actually, the way Ignatius uses the parable of the king to help fire up the imagination of the retreatant for the person of Jesus seems to have been the way the early Christians used the Suffering Servant stories of Isaiah to catch the imagination of their hearers. One can imagine them saying to one another: "Remember the story of the Suffering Servant in Isaiah? Well, in Jesus that story has come true, and in spades!"

Let me underline an important point here. Ignatius did not become a totally different person with this first discernment and his conversion. He was the same ambitious, driven man.[41] From his own experience Ignatius learned how God could use his imaginative powers to teach him and draw him to a new way of life. We have already seen how the insight he gained from his daydreams during his convalescence was probably the kernel of the kingdom meditation which he puts at the beginning of that part of the *Spiritual Exercises* given over to contemplating the public life of Jesus. It is aimed to fire the imagination with desire to know Jesus better in order to love him more and follow him more closely. But Ignatius also learned that God uses the gospel stories to draw us imaginatively into their world in order to reveal himself to us. So let us look at some of the suggestions Ignatius makes in the Exercises.

Let me use the two contemplations of the incarnation and the nativity. Here Ignatius spells out the suggestions that will apply for all the contemplations to come. In the Second Prelude of all the contemplations of the life of Christ, Ignatius suggests "a composition, by imagining the place." In the contemplation of the incarnation he says: "Here it will be to see the great extent of the circuit of the world, with peoples so many and so diverse; and then to see in particular the house and rooms of Our Lady, in the city of Nazareth in the province of Galilee" (n. 103). Immediately we see that Ignatius goes well beyond the gospel text in his suggestions for the imagination.

In the text of the contemplation itself he fleshes out the panoramic view of the world to have us picture the Trinity "gazing on the whole face and circuit of the earth" (n. 106). The imaginative breadth is enormous, the whole sweep of the earth under the gaze of God, and then it narrows to a tiny village in the backwater province of Galilee and there to the home of a young girl. The three points ask the retreatant to "see the various persons, some here, some there," to "listen to what the persons on the face of the earth are saying," "what the Divine Persons are saying," "what the angel and Our Lady are saying," and then to "consider what the people on the face of the earth are doing," "what the Divine Persons are doing," "what the angel and Our Lady are doing." Nowhere in the gospels do we have any mention of what is going on in the rest of the world at the time of the annunciation, nor do we read of the counsels of the Holy Trinity. Yet Ignatius imagines what is behind the text. The Trinity must have taken counsel together, and for a reason. The reason, he imagines, is what they see in the world, namely, that people are going to hell and something needs to be done. Ignatius believes that if we let our imaginations go in this way God will reveal to us who Jesus is and what he stands for so that we will fall in love with him and want to follow him.

The Nativity contemplation repeats the suggestion about the composition, imagining the place.

> Here it will be to see in imagination the road from Nazareth to Bethlehem. Consider its length and breadth, whether it is level or winds through valleys and hills. Similarly, look at the place or cave of the Nativity: How big is it, or small? How low or high? And how is it furnished? (n. 112)

Ignatius gives free rein to the retreatant's imagination. Even though he had been to the Holy Land, he does not tell the retreatant how the terrain looks in reality. Each retreatant is free to imagine what the terrain and place might look like. In the contemplation proper he again counsels looking at the persons, listening to what they say, and considering what they are doing. He also adds a new person to the scene, a "maidservant," and suggests that "I will make myself a poor, little, and unworthy slave, gazing at them, contemplating them, and serving them in their needs, just as if I were there" (n. 114). Such suggestions have freed retreatants to imagine themselves in the scene in many ways. Women act as midwives; one pediatrician helped Mary to deliver Jesus and then held him in his arms and handed him to Mary. We can see that Ignatius expects that God will fulfill the desire of the retreatant to get to know Jesus more intimately through the use of his or her imagination.

This is probably as good a place as any to discuss at more length the issue of imagination and fantasy in prayer. In the history of spirituality there have been two main ways of prayer. One way stresses imageless, quiet prayer. In our day this way is perhaps best exemplified by the use of centering prayer. One of the best known teachers of this kind of prayer in the United States is the Cistercian monk, Basil Pennington.[42] In Great Britain and many other English-speaking countries the late Benedictine, John Main, has had and continues to have a wide influence.[43] It is a very helpful way of giving ourselves a chance to get in touch with the Mystery we call God at the center of our being. The other way is exemplified by the Ignatian tradition which advocates using all of our faculties in prayer: sensation, imagination, mind, will. The stress on this way in this book should not be taken to mean that this way is normative for everyone. Both traditions have a venerable history, and I suspect that most people can be helped to meet God by trying both ways. It could be that some kinds of personalities prefer one way to the other, but I am not prepared to try to distinguish personality types and their affinities for prayer forms. I would encourage people to use whatever helps them to meet the living God. Methods are only means to that desired end. When the end is attained, i.e., when God is encountered, then the relationship itself takes over.

But we need to say something about the use of imagination as a method that many have found very helpful in meeting God. We let the words of a gospel scene touch our imaginations in much the same way that poetry or a novel might, asking the Lord to reveal himself to us in the process. We can imagine ourselves as actually a part of the scene, as Ignatius suggests.

At different times in our lives we will find ourselves identifying more with one character than another in a gospel scene. When, for example, we feel lost and unsure of our path, we may identify with Bartimaeus, the blind beggar of Mark 10, who cries out, even against opposition, "Jesus, son of David, have mercy on me!" The opposition may be within us, in the inner voice that tries to tell us that prayer is futile. Then we, too, may have to cry out all the more, and we, too, may hear deep within us Jesus saying, "What do you want me to do for you?" And we respond with our need to see, "My Teacher, let me see again; let me see my way." And then we can pour out our heart's pain to him.

At another time we may find ourselves surprised at our reactions to a gospel scene. One man, for example, was reading the section in Mark 3 where it says, "He went up the mountain and called to him those whom he wanted; and they came to him. And he appointed twelve, whom he also named apostles, to be with him, and to be sent out to proclaim the message, and to have authority to cast out demons" (Mk 3:13–15). He found himself getting angry, and he did not understand why. He asked the Lord to help him to understand what was happening. Gradually it dawned on him that a Christian does not have much choice of who his companions are going to be. He realized that he was angry at a number of the people with whom his Christian living had brought him together. The resentment had been building up unawares and affecting his happiness and his effectiveness in work. The realization in itself freed him of some of his anger, and he was also able to ask Jesus to help him to look at his companions as also Jesus' companions.

Another example: People are often surprised at how difficult it is to let Jesus wash their feet as he washed the feet of his disciples at the last supper (Jn 13). When they recoil, they now understand Peter's reaction which before had seemed incomprehensible. As they ponder their reaction and ask the Lord's light on it, they come to sense that their real sin is the unwillingness to accept Jesus' forgiveness and to believe that they are loved and, therefore, lovable.

People obviously differ in their imaginative abilities, or perhaps better, in the kinds of imagination they have. Some seem able to visualize in colorful detail the whole gospel scene, almost as though their imaginations were creating a Technicolor movie. Others have a vivid auditory imagination so that whole conversations seem to go on in their heads and hearts. Others, and here I count myself, do not seem to see or hear much at all, but to feel the story and the characters in a way that is hard to describe. This last group can be envious when they listen to the more vivid descriptions of others and may even feel discouraged at their "lack of imagination." Actually everyone has an imagination. If you wince when someone describes the impact of a hammer hitting his thumb, you have an imagination; if you can enjoy a good story, you have an imagination. Imaginations differ; we need to let God use the one we have and not bemoan the one we do not have.

There are some people with vivid, creative imaginations who have been able to let God use this gift as a way to develop the relationship. One woman I know spent the good part of a retreat on a vacation with Jesus during which time she was able to pour out her heart to him and ask his advice about how to handle some of the troubling issues of her life. Some of her times of prayer were spent imaginatively outdoors, some before a fireplace. Near the end of the retreat Jesus left and headed back to the city, and she knew that this was his way of telling her that he would be with her in her daily life. One man spent a long time in prayer on a camping trip with Jesus. In the course of the trip the basic issue of their relationship emerged, namely the man's ability and willingness to trust Jesus enough to tell him what was really on his mind. Some people create whole stories out of incidents in the gospels. One woman followed Jesus on the way of the cross in vivid detail, even to the point of helping him to his feet when he stumbled and staying close to him when the guards became menacing and tried to drive her away. Nothing could keep her from going with Jesus.

When we use our imaginations in prayer in any of these ways, we are aware that much of what happens is our own product, based on our own past experience. How can we be sure that the whole thing is not just a fanciful daydream that we piously call prayer? My first answer is a trust in tradition. God has, it seems, used the imagination of saints like Ignatius of Loyola, Francis Xavier, Margaret Mary Alacoque to draw them into a very deep intimate friendship with him. Then I would point to a need for discernment, but a discernment that does not take as a starting point suspicion of our human nature, but trust that God has made us good. It is a profound insight of Ignatius to note in the beginning of his rules for discernment that God's presence to those who are searching for him is signaled by positive emotions: gentleness, peacefulness, quiet confidence (nn. 315–316). If our use of the imagination leads to such feelings as well as to an increased faith and hope and love, and a desire to know God and Jesus more, then we can have confidence that the Lord is using our imaginations for his purposes and our good. Doubts about such prayer can be seen as temptations, especially if the doubts and questions allow of no clear answers, that is, remain only as nagging doubts and questions and do not lead to new and better ways to pray.

In this matter of discernment it also helps to have someone we can talk to about our prayer. That is, it is good to have a spiritual director.[44] For now it suffices to note that it is very helpful for retreatants' confidence in the direction of their prayer life to be able to describe what is happening to someone who is interested in listening to it. Just the act of describing to another what happens when they pray helps them to be more attentive to the conscious relationship with God and more appreciative of the gifts they have been given, even if the other person does nothing more than listen attentively and sympathetically. In the process of describing their experience they often see where they are being led by God and where they are straying from the path. It is even more helpful, of course, if the spiritual director can also, by judicious questions and comments, help retreatants to see that their prayer is leading toward a deeper intimacy with the Lord that fits the pattern of how God has dealt with people, even if each person is a unique exemplar of the pattern.

The main point of this chapter is to encourage directors to be as free as Ignatius in encouraging retreatants to use whatever helps them to meet the living God. In the Ignatian tradition imagination has been a great help. If this is their way, let them trust it as one of God's gifts to help them to know God better.

7

THE DISCERNMENT OF SPIRITS

Ignatius of Loyola lived in an age comparable in its turmoil and promise to our own. He, too, lived on the cusp as one world order crumbled and a new one was struggling to be born. One could say that he was one of the religious geniuses the Catholic Church needed at that time to see its way into the new world being born during his lifetime. His genius lay in realizing that God can be found in all things, that every human experience has a religious dimension, has religious meaning, for those who want to discover it. This discovery of the religious meaning of one's inner experience is called the discernment of spirits, a term that was rich in tradition long before the life of Ignatius, but one which received new impetus and use with the publication of the *Spiritual Exercises*. In this book Ignatius codified the "Rules for the Discernment of Spirits" which he learned from his own experience (nn. 313–336). But because discernment of spirits is often viewed as an arcane and mysterious process, something left to the mystics and masters of spirituality, we need to look more closely at this process to see how it can become an ordinary event in the life of any Christian.

Ignatius' Own Discernment

In the last chapter we referred to the first discernment of spirits Ignatius fell into. He noticed that two sets of daydreams led to different affective states, and he drew the conclusion that God was leading him toward a new way of life, away from the life of chivalry which gave him so much apparent pleasure. The interesting point about this first discernment is that it occurred to a layman quite innocent of any theological or spiritual knowledge. Moreover, it happened in the ordinary event of daydreaming. Nothing could be further from the esoteric or mystical as these are ordinarily understood. Thus, we have in this story a description of the discernment of spirits in ordinary life, a description that lays to rest any theory of the discernment of spirits that makes it an esoteric or arcane spiritual discipline open only to the spiritually gifted and theologically trained. Ignatius was theologically ignorant, and was so far from being spiritually gifted that even after this first discernment and a vision of the Madonna he could not make up his mind about whether to kill a Moor or not, as the story from the next chapter of his autobiography attests.

Right after he left Loyola to take up his new life of following Jesus, he and a Moor met on the road, both riding mules. They began to converse and the conversation turned to the topic of Mary, the mother of Jesus. The Moor could well imagine that Mary had conceived Jesus without benefit of a man, but he could not agree that she was a virgin after giving birth. Ignatius tried to dissuade him from this opinion, but could not succeed. The Autobiography tells us that the Moor raced on ahead of Ignatius. We can imagine that the Moor felt Ignatius getting more and more irate. After the Moor left, Ignatius began to have misgivings about his behavior; perhaps he had not done enough to uphold the honor of Our Lady. The desire came over him to race after the Moor and strike him with his dagger. He couldn't make up his mind. He couldn't discern what to do, in other words. And he was in an agony of indecision. Finally in desperation he decided to let the mule make the decision for him. He let the reins go slack. If the mule followed the broad road to the town to which the Moor was heading, Ignatius would seek him and strike him; if the mule kept to the road he was on, then he would let the Moor go. The mule kept to the road he was on.[45]

Obviously Ignatius did not immediately become a master of discernment.

Nonetheless, with the first discernment he made on his sickbed, we have the essential elements for an understanding of Ignatian discernment. Life is a battleground where the stakes are enormous. The two great protagonists in this battle are God and Satan. Both are in a dialogical relationship with all human beings, but for absolutely different ends. God wants all human beings to live as God's sons and daughters, as brothers and sisters of Jesus Christ. In other words, God wants all human beings to be saved, and God is working all the time in this world to achieve that end. Satan diametrically opposes God's purpose. He wants to estrange all human beings not only from God but also from one another. The battlegrounds are the hearts and minds of human beings. Thus, for Ignatius, the struggle is dialogical; God is trying to attract human beings to enter the community life of the Trinity, and Satan is trying to draw us away from that community. In ordinary human experience both God and the Evil One are at their work of attracting us. Hence, in ordinary human experience the influences of the two great protagonists can be discerned. Nothing in human experience is, for Ignatius, insignificant, because at every moment God and Satan are at work. Careful attention to inner experience, therefore, is a hallmark of Ignatian spirituality; such attention is absolutely necessary if the individual wants to know God's desires for him or her.

This aspect of Ignatius' spirituality has great relevance for our own age, when many of the institutions, structures and customs by which people lived their lives without much thought have been called into question. There are few outside criteria by which men and women of today can make clear decisions about right and wrong, or about the better way to live their lives. Moreover, as John Macmurray long ago pointed out, our civilization has arrived at the point where our intellects are refined and highly honed but our emotions (our hearts) are relatively undeveloped and immature. In a trenchant series of B.B.C. broadcasts in the early 1930's he argued forcefully that western-ers needed to submit to the discipline of developing more adult and civilized hearts.[46] I have developed his thoughts and tried to show that the discernment of spirits is a primary way to attain that maturity of heart.[47] The genius of this sixteenth century saint, Ignatius of Loyola, still has relevance for our day.

However, another aspect of this spirituality may be much more difficult for modern men and women to accept. At Manresa, Ignatius was tutored by God and gradually became a master of discernment. During these months of prayer he became convinced that God wanted him to live out his days in Jerusalem, and with the single-mindedness so characteristic of him he proceeded to go there. "He made a firm decision to remain in Jerusalem, constantly visiting the Holy Places. In addition to this devout desire of his, he was also intent on help-ing souls."[48] When the provincial of the Franciscans told him that he could not remain, Ignatius told him quite frankly that he was determined to stay. Only when the provincial threatened him with excommunication did Ignatius agree to obey, conclud-ing that "it was not Our Lord's will for him to remain in the Holy Places...."[49]

One commentator on the rules for discernment, Leo Bakker, maintains that the decision to remain in Jerusalem was made around the time of the vision by the river Cardoner and was an election in the "first time," that is, "an occasion when God our Lord moves and attracts the will in such a way that a devout person, without doubting or being able to doubt, carries out what was proposed" (Sp. Ex. #175). According to Bakker, the decision of the provincial in Jerusalem posed to Ignatius the question of trying to figure out how a decision clearly God's (his election to stay in Jerusalem) could be contrary to a decision clearly God's (the provincial's decision). In Bakker's view reflection on this question led to the eighth rule of the rules for discernment appropriate to the Second Week of the Exercises

(#336) in which Ignatius cautions the exercitant to distinguish carefully the moment of a consolation without previous cause from succeeding moments.[50] Bakker also traces the Rules for Thinking with the Church in the *Spiritual Exercises* (nn.352–370) to this experience in Jerusalem. For Ignatius, authority in the church was clearly a mediator of the will of God. Discernment of spirits was always in creative tension with obedience to legitimate authority as a means of knowing God's will. For many modern Christians, Catholics among them, authority does not have the same sharp relevance that it had for Ignatius. Many would find inexplicable the complete acquiescence of a man of such obvious strength of character to the provincial's authority. Yet Ignatian discernment must be understood as embedded in the "Catholic thing," in the belief that the institutional church also mediates the will of God. Ignation spirituality is decidedly realistic and Catholic. Discernment takes place in the real world where all things are not possible and in the Catholic Church where legitimate authority may have the final word.

Discernment and the "Principle and Foundation"

Now let us develop at more length some of the central elements of Ignatian discernment of spirits. First, the discernment of spirits must be understood against the background of the First Principle and Foundation, "The Fundamentum" elucidated by Joseph Tetlow.[51] Tetlow argues that behind the seemingly dry and catechism-like words of Ignatius, as we have argued in chapter 4, lies an experience of God's creative and continually creating action. I have found the philosophy of action of the Scottish philosopher John Macmurray particularly helpful in understanding what Ignatius intended with the Fundamentum.[52] Macmurray comes to the conclusion that the universe is the one action of God, an action governed by one intention. We only know anyone's intention through that person's revelation; *a for-*

tiori we can only know God's intention through revelation. Christians believe that God has revealed God's intention in Christ Jesus. At the least we can say that God has revealed God's intention for our world, whatever may be said of the whole universe. "God's intention, it seems, is that all human beings live as brothers and sisters in a community of faith, hope and love united with Jesus Christ as sons and daughters of God, our Father and in harmony with the whole created universe.[53] I have argued elsewhere that this one action of God can be understood as the kingdom of God, the central theme of the preaching Jesus.[54] God is always actively bringing about God's kingdom, and we can be in tune with God's intention, out of tune or more or less in tune. With absolute clarity and consequentiality Ignatius saw that for our own best interests and blessedness we need to be in tune with God's one action. The First Principle and Foundation is a pithy statement of this insight. Let me paraphrase the first two sentences of the Principle in the language of this chapter. "Human beings are created for community with the Trinity and hence with one another. All the other things on the face of the earth are created to help us to attain this community." We have to understand this statement not as an external demand put on human beings by a sovereign and implacable God, but as an expression of what is for our good. The *Spiritual Exercises* are a means to become attuned to God's one action and intention, to become contemplatives in action, people who quite literally find God in all things even in the hurly-burly of a very active life.

Discernment and Action

Historically the purpose of the Exercises has been understood in two different senses. One tendency stressed the aim of union with God; the other stressed the discovery of God's will. With Bakker and other modern commentators, I prefer to join the two and see the *Spiritual Exercises* as a means of helping exercitants to union with God in action. Bakker notes, for example, that for Ignatius, consolation was not first and foremost a pleasant and moving emotion nor encouragement to continue on a chosen path nor help in prayer; consolation includes all of these, but first and foremost it is an experience that makes it possible to know and choose the will of God.

> From the time of the illumination at Cardoner the discernment of inner movements and consolation flow together with the election (e.g., the choice of a way of life) for Ignatius. The fact that Ignatius reflexively emphasizes this flowing together of consolation and election and then methodically works it out as the center and source of the spiritual life is the new element brought into the history of spirituality by the *Spiritual Exercises*.[55]

In other words, in Ignation spirituality union with God occurs in the decision to act in a certain way and in the action itself. In Macmurray's terminology, we become one with God insofar as we are in tune with the one action of God in our own actions. To put it another way, we become one with God insofar as our actions are in tune with the kingdom of God.[56]

In the *Autobiography* Ignatius tells us that he learned to distrust consolations that came to him as he was about to go to sleep. These consolations kept him from the little sleep he had allotted to himself.

> Now and then reflecting on this loss of sleep, he considered how he had allotted a fixed amount of time each day to converse with God, and then the remainder of the day as well, and thus he came to doubt whether those lights came from the good spirit. He concluded that it was better to set them aside and sleep the allotted time. This he did.[57]

Later, in Barcelona and in Paris, he found that consolations kept him from paying attention in class or from memorizing his grammar lessons. Gradually he came to the conclusion that these consolations were temptations.[58] In these two vignettes Ignatius shows how deeply he has penetrated the mystery of God's unitive action in this world. Even profound spiritual consolations can be discovered as temptations by reference to their deleterious effects on action which one has discerned to be in tune with God's one action. Asceticism requires that one eschew such consolations in order to be in union with God.

For Ignatius the discernment of spirits became so important in ordinary life that he frequently made examens of consciousness.[59] Moreover, he would allow a Jesuit to miss all other spiritual exercises for the sake of the apostolate except the examen of consciousness. For Ignatius, as I have argued elsewhere,[60] the examen functioned much as the period of reflection after each prayer time in the *Spiritual Exercises*. Just as the exercitant is asked to reflect on the period of prayer to discern the movements of the spirits so, too, for Ignatius, the contemplative in action, a period of the day could be considered a time of encountering the different spirits, and so he reflected on that period to discover the movements of these spirits.

Rules for Discernment

For our own good God desires that each of us be in tune with his one action in our actions; in our best moments we, too, desire to be in tune with God's action. How do we know whether we are in tune or not? I believe that when we are out of tune with God's one action, we experience ourselves as alienated, unhappy, unfulfilled, even though we do not know the source of the malaise. These feelings of malaise are, I believe, what Ignatius calls the actions of the "good spirit" in his first rule for the discernment of spirits.

> In the case of persons who are going from one mortal sin to another, the enemy ordinarily proposes apparent pleasures. He makes them imagine delights and pleasures of the senses, in order to hold them fast and plunge them deeper into their sins and vices.
>
> But with persons of this type the good spirit uses a contrary procedure. Through their good judgment on problems of morality he stings their consciences with remorse (Sp. Ex., #314).

In other words, when I am out of tune with the one action of God, when I am acting predominantly out of fear for myself and, therefore, against the community of the Trinity, rather than out of love for others, then I experience the action of God as a troubling of my spirit, as a sting of conscience. Ignatius' own experience of sadness after the daydreams about knightly deeds is an example of this action of God. God continually acts in the universe to draw all of us into community with the Trinity and with one another. When we act counter to that action, we experience ourselves as somehow out of sorts with ourselves and with others. In this understanding there is no need of special interventions by God or the good spirit although we may experience the one action of God as an external intervention.

The second rule for the discernment of spirits in the Exercises speaks "of persons who are earnestly purging away their sins, and who are progressing from good to better in the service of God our Lord." In our terminology these are people who desire to attune their actions with the one action of God and desire it effectively. In this case, Ignatius says,

> ...it is characteristic of the evil spirit to cause gnawing anxiety, to sadden, and to set up obstacles. In this he unsettles these persons by false reasons aimed at preventing their progress.
>
> But with persons of this type it is characteristic of the

good spirit to stir up courage and strength, consolations, tears, inspirations, and tranquillity. He makes things easier and eliminates all obstacles, so that the persons may move forward in doing good (Sp. Ex., 315).

Can we make sense of this for our times? In an earlier book I answered the question in this way:

If you have ever experienced a time when you were "in the flow," able to live with relative unambivalence and lack of fear in the now, attuned to the presence of God, then you have an idea of what it might be like to be at one with the one action of God. In such a state you are a contemplative in action. You know that you are at the right place at the right time. There are no doubts about whether you should be someone else or somewhere else. You do not need to justify being married or single or a religious; it is right to be who you are here and now. And you live and act comfortably with the knowledge of your own limitations, of your finitude, of your small part in the immense history of the world. To be attuned to the one action of God, to his will, is to be extraordinarily free, happy and fulfilled even in the midst of a world of sorrow and pain. One can, perhaps, understand how Jesus could celebrate the Last Supper even though he knew in his bones that it would be "last." [61]

To be in tune with God's intention in this way is to experience what Ignatius calls "consolation" in the next rule:

By [this kind of] consolation I mean that which occurs when some interior motion is caused within the soul through which it comes to be inflamed with

love of its Creator and Lord. As a result it can love
no created thing on the face of the earth in itself, but
only in the Creator of them all.

Similarly, this consolation is experienced when the
soul sheds tears which move it to love for its Lord—
whether they are tears of grief for its own sins, or
about the Passion of Christ our Lord, or about other
matters directly ordered to his service and praise.

Finally, under the word consolation I include every
increase in faith, hope, and charity, and every interior
joy which calls and attracts toward heavenly things
and to the salvation of one's soul, by bringing it tranquillity and peace in its Creator and Lord (Sp. Ex.,
316.).

With Josef Sudbrack we can equate the modern concept of
identity with Ignatius' concept of consolation.[62] According to
this theory the best criterion for discerning whether we are in
tune with God's one action in our daily choices is the sense of
developing inner and outer harmony, a growing sense of ourselves as related harmoniously to other people, our world and
our God. A person who has come to an habitual way of discerning in this way is well on the way to being a contemplative in
action.

To be out of tune with God's intention is to experience
what Ignatius calls "desolation" in the fourth rule:

By [this kind of] desolation I mean everything which
is contrary of what was described in the Third Rule;
for example, obtuseness of soul, turmoil within it, an
impulsive motion toward low and earthly things, or
disquiet from various agitations and temptations.
These move one toward lack of faith and leave one
without hope and without love. One is completely

listless, tepid, and unhappy, and feels separated from
our Creator and Lord (317).

I believe that it is easy enough to recognize such desolation
when its source is personal sinfulness, when the person is personally alienated from God's intention. What directors need to
be alert to is the possibility that such "desolation" comes from a
sense of hopelessness about our social lives. The attitude of
alienation from institutions is all-pervasive in our society. We
see corruption all around us, in government, in business, even in
the churches. There is a wholesale lack of trust not only of "City
Hall" (meaning any institution that governs), but also of fellow
citizens. Crime in the streets, in schools, in our homes, is an
everyday affair. Anger and hatred often seem only barely con-
cealed, and violence only with great control avoided. Many, if
not most, of us experience a sense of frustration and helplessness about the structures and patterns that govern our lives. We
may also vaguely feel a complicity in these structures or patterns. For example, race and class seem to keep so many of our
fellow citizens trapped in the inner cities of our country. We
become aware of the possibility that we ourselves are part of the
problem, not of the solution. Such feelings can make prayer very
difficult, if not impossible.

However, if these feelings do not lead to a deeper conversation with the Lord and to a concerted effort to do our part to
change the sinful social structures that condition our lives as a
people, then they are "desolation," what I would call, for lack of
a better word, "social desolation." When we encounter such desolation in ourselves or in our directees, we need to bring these
feelings of helplessness and lack of hope to the Lord for healing.
At a meeting in Brussels on the *Spiritual Exercises,* Gerard W.
Hughes, S.J. made a very interesting observation. He has found
that people who have spent time working for social justice often
feel, during the First Week, "shame and confusion" (what they
desire in the First Week, n. 48) because of the sorry state of the

society they are part of. Interestingly enough, this shame and confusion is liberating; they discover that God does not want society to be so unjust, but that God still loves the world and this society and wants people who will help to change it.

An Example That Illustrates the Use of the Rules

It would take us too far afield to go through all the Rules for Discernment in the *Spiritual Exercises*. What I wanted to show here is that these rules are not esoteric and out of the ordinary. They can be verified in our ordinary lives if we take the time to pay attention to our experience. However, a recent novel, *Glamorous Powers*, by Susan Howatch might well be read as a description of the discernment of spirits. It reads like a spiritual mystery story.

Two of Ignatius' rules can be illustrated by one section of the novel. The protagonist is Father Darrow, an abbot of the Fordite Congregation noted for his psychic and spiritual gifts (the "glamorous powers" of the title). On the occasion of the death of the founder of the Fordites, Darrow's mentor, and the accession to the office of Abbot-General of his rival, Father Francis, Darrow has a vision which he interprets as a call to leave the Fordites and return to life as a priest in the "world." Abbot Francis, however, has doubts about the authenticity of the call and demands that Darrow enter into a period of discernment with him. Darrow tries to use his psychic powers and his self-control to bend the process of discernment toward his interpretation of the vision. He lies, in fact. In Rule Thirteen of the Rules for the First Week (n.326) Ignatius notes that the bad spirit tries to seduce the directee into secrecy about what is actually happening in his or her experience. In Rule One of the Rules for the Second Week he notes that "it is characteristic of the enemy to fight against this happiness and spiritual consolation, by using specious reasons, subtleties, and persistent deceits" (n. 329). In his attempts to sidetrack an authentic discernment of spirits,

Darrow becomes an angry and very unhappy man. The turn toward real discernment comes in the following scene. Darrow is narrating.

"I lied to you yesterday," I said to Francis when we met again. "I'm sorry. I know very well I've got to be entirely truthful in order to help you reach the right decision."

Francis never asked what the lie was. That impressed me. Nor did he make any attempt to humiliate me further by embarking on a justifiable reproof. That impressed me even more. Instead he motioned me to sit down and said abruptly:

"It's a question of trust, isn't it, and you don't trust me yet."

I forced myself to say: "I do want to trust you."

"Well, at least that's a step in the right direction."

"And I do accept that you're a first-class monk-"

"No, you don't. You accept that I'm a first-class administrator and you accept that the old man gave me a first-class training, but I've still to prove I'm a first-class monk, and that's why it's just as vital for me as it is for you that I should deal with your crisis correctly. I know perfectly well that you believe the only reason why I became Abbot-General was because I knew how to exploit the old man's secret longing for a son. Well, now I have to prove the old man wasn't completely off his head and that I really am the right man for the job, so accept that I have a powerful motive to behave properly here, Jonathan, and do please discard your fear that I'll be unable to wield the charism of discernment unless you regularly throw in a lie or two to help me along."

Yet again I was impressed. I heard myself say: "It takes courage to be as honest as that. Thank you. I can't promise you I'll succeed in matching your honesty, but I can promise I'll do my best to try."

"Then put on your boxing-gloves," said Francis, not ill-pleased by this exchange, "and let's step back into the ring for the next round."[63]

The novel as a whole concerns the struggle of Darrow to discern the meaning of his vocation.

Conclusion

On his sickbed Ignatius had two sets of daydreams which had different repercussions in his emotional life. One day he noticed the difference and then decided that one set of daydreams was from God, the other not. Yet God was also in the worldly daydreams, as the spirit that left him feeling disconsolate afterwards. From these simple beginnings Ignatian spirituality developed. Ignatius learned from experience that God could be found in all things. The phrase "finding God in all things" has become a hallmark of Ignatian spirituality. What Ignatius learned on his sickbed and later is part of the heritage of the church's tradition. It still has relevance for our own time. We need only begin to pay attention to our experience and to ask where God is present in it.

8

THE CHANGING SELF-GOD IMAGE OF
IGNATIUS OF LOYOLA
IN RELATION TO DISCERNMENT

Since the assimilation of modern psychology into contemporary spirituality, we have become accustomed to describing the developing relationship of a person with God in interpersonal terms. I have tried such a description in *Spiritual Direction and the Encounter with God* where I described prayer as conscious relationship and then attempted to describe the development of that relationship in terms of the dynamic of the *Spiritual Exercises*.[64] Those of us who use such a framework often use a form of what Freudians call "object relations theory" and apply it to the relationship with God.[65] According to this theory, we all carry around with us self-other schemata (internal "images" or psychic structures of the self in relation to others) learned in our interactions with significant people. With these schemata we approach all new people. Such a theory serves to explain instant likes and dislikes. A new person is assimilated into an image of someone in my past life whom I liked or disliked. The theory is also used to explain how people get into repetitive destructive relationships without ever learning from experience. These schemata are self-other psychic structures; they are relational in nature because they are learned through relationships. In other words, the images with their associated feelings and thoughts are of the self in relation to another and others. All our images of self are relational.

According to this theory, we also meet God with learned

self-God schemata which derive from our relationships with parents and others, from teachings about God, and from past experiences of the Mystery we call God.[66] These schemata are always distorted and untrue to the reality of who God really is for us. In other words, our experience of God is impoverished because of our self-God schemata. We could say that the development of the relationship with God consists in the learning of progressively more realistic images of self and God in relationship through the actual encounter with God in sacraments, prayer, and life in general. The development could be seen as a process of losing our idols or false images of God (and self) through the encounter itself, just as the actual encounter with a new person in our life will teach us something new about ourselves and that person if we let the relationship develop.

I contend that one criterion for assessing whether retreatants or directees are heading in the right direction in their lives might be to help them to look at the quality of the relationship with God and the changes that have taken place in the relationship. Thus shifts in a certain direction in a person's self-God schema could be used to discern whether certain experiences are of God or not, and whether the thrust of a person's life is moving forward or regressing.

In this chapter I want to illustrate such a progression by using the *Autobiography* of Ignatius. I believe that the experiences Ignatius describes in the first three chapters of that work can be understood in terms of Ignatius' progressive education about his relationship with God. In other words, the changes he describes can be understood as changes in his self-God schema. In the course of demonstrating this thesis we will discover that Ignatius, who calls himself the pilgrim in the *Autobiography*, shows himself to be a pilgrim from an impoverished image of God to an image of God as Lover *par excellence*. In the process his own self-image changes as well.

First, let us once again note that Ignatius' initial conversion experience came about through noticing the difference between two sets of daydreams as he convalesced from his wounds and the leg operations those wounds entailed. In one set of daydreams Ignatius spent hours on end imagining the great deeds he would do, the fine words he would say to win the heart of a great lady. In the other set Ignatius spent equally long hours dreaming of the great deeds he would do for Christ in imitation of saints like Dominic and Francis. He notes that there was a difference in the two experiences:

> When he thought of worldly matters he found much delight, but after growing weary and dismissing them he found that he was dry and unhappy. But when he thought of going barefoot to Jerusalem and of eating nothing but vegetables and of imitating the saints in all the austerities they performed, he not only found consolation in these thoughts but even after they had left him he remained happy and joyful. He did not consider nor did he stop to examine this difference until one day his eyes were partially opened and he began to wonder at this difference and to reflect upon it. From experience he knew that some thoughts left him sad while others made him happy, and little by little he came to perceive the different spirits that were moving him; one coming from the devil, the other coming from God.[67]

In these two sets of daydreams the same vaulting ambition, the same vivid imagination are at work, but to different ends. The reading of the life of Christ and of the lives of the saints piqued Ignatius' interest and fired his imagination much as did the romantic literature he so enjoyed and would have preferred to read during his convalescence. Finally, he noticed that the two sets of daydreams had different emotional consequences in his heart, and then he discerned that one set is from God, the other from the demon.

With this decisive discernment Ignatius was set upon a new path, but he was not yet a new person. The rather amusing story of his encounter with the Moor on the road to Montserrat, recounted earlier, shows how far he was from being a man of discernment.[68] What was Ignatius' image of himself in relation to God at this time? A telling phrase occurs in the passage where he recounts his desire to enter the Carthusian house in Seville.

> But when he again thought of the penances he want-
> ed to fulfill as he went about the world, the desire for
> the Carthusian way of life cooled since he feared that
> there he would not be able to give vent to the *hatred*
> that he had conceived against himself.[69]

That self-hatred tells us much about his image of God at this time of preparation for the journey that would end up in Manresa. If Ignatius hates himself so violently, we can speculate that he harbors an image of himself before an implacable God. Not long after his arrival in Manresa we hear ominous hints of where such a self-God image can lead.

> While in Manresa he begged alms every day. He ate
> no meat, nor did he drink wine, though both were
> offered to him. On Sundays he did not fast, and if
> someone gave him wine, he drank it. And because he
> had been quite meticulous in caring for his hair,
> which was according to the fashion of the day —and
> he had a good crop of hair—he decided to let it grow
> naturally without combing, cutting, or covering it
> with anything either during the day or night. For the
> same reason he let the nails of his feet and hands
> grow since he had also been overly neat with regard
> to them.[70]

He began to attack his body and his former attitudes with reckless abandon to the point where he did permanent harm to his health, as he notes later. It is at this point that he mentions the serpent-like image that "gave him much consolation." "He received much delight and consolation from gazing upon this object and the more he looked upon it, the more his consolation increased, but when the object vanished he became disconsolate."[71] Ignatius did not make the connection with the earlier discernment when he noted that the daydreams of doing knightly deeds delighted him during the dreaming, but left him sad afterward. Moreover, he notes that around the time when this vision began, "a disturbing thought came to torment him, pointing out to him the burdensomeness of his life. It was like someone speaking within his soul: 'And how will you be able to put up with this for the seventy years you have ahead of you?'"[72] With this temptation began the great swings of mood which led him into the terrible bout of scruples which he so poignantly describes in the following pages of the *Autobiography*.

The agony of his struggle with these scruples brought him to this point:

> Once, being very disturbed because of them, he set himself to pray and with great fervor he cried aloud to God, saying, "Help me, Lord, for I find no remedy among men, nor in any creature. No task would be too irksome for me if I thought I could get help. Lord, show me where I may get it, and even if I have to follow after a little dog to get the remedy I need, I will do it."
> Taken up with these thoughts he was many times vehemently tempted to throw himself into a deep hole in his room which was near the place where he used to pray.[73]

His self-hatred has taken a very violent turn. What kind of

image of God lies behind such scruples? It has to be a God who, in the words of the psychiatrist J. S. Mackenzie cited earlier, "is always snooping around after sinners."[74] Ignatius felt that he had not completely confessed his sins. At one point a confessor ordered him not to confess any sins of the past "unless it was something abundantly clear. But since he considered everything manifestly clear, the order benefited him not at all..."[75] For Ignatius at this time God must have been a terrible judge ready to pounce on every sin.

Finally, Ignatius had a couple of days in which he felt free from scruples:

> But on the third day, which was Tuesday, the remembrance of his sins returned to him while he was at prayer, and as one thing leads to another, he thought of sin after sin from his past life and felt obliged to confess them again. After these thoughts, there came upon him a loathing for the life he was then living and he had a strong temptation to give it up. In this manner the Lord chose to awaken him as from a dream.[76]

Ignatius, we can speculate, has realized that the image of God with which he has operated thus far in Manresa was a product of the demon, and not an image of the true God. He continues:

> Now that he had some experience with the different spirits—through the lessons that God had given him—he began to think about the way that that spirit had come to him. Thus he decided, and with great clarity of mind, never to confess his past sins again and from that day forward he was free of his scruples, and he held it for certain that Our Lord had desired to set him free because of his mercy.[77]

God is not implacable, but merciful, and Ignatius can count on this God. Thus he need not continually grub around in his mind for possible unconfessed sins.

Immediately after recounting this discernment Ignatius describes how he rather easily discerned God's will in two matters which before would have led to agonizing indecision. The first we have already mentioned, namely, how he came to realize that great spiritual consolations at bed time were a temptation and not of God.[78] How his image of God has changed! In the next paragraph he describes how an experience of the image of meat compelled him to abandon, without any hesitation or doubt, his firm practice of never eating meat. Even when his confessor asked him to consider whether this was a temptation, Ignatius could not doubt that the good spirit was the source of the image. He then says: "During this period God was dealing with him in the same way a schoolteacher deals with a child while instructing him."[79] He then goes on to describe in five points the ways God revealed himself, culminating in the description of the extraordinary enlightenment on the banks of the Cardoner. After this experience he recognized the image of the serpent-like figure as a temptation.

The final demonstration that the encounter with God changed Ignatius' self-God schema comes from the very next paragraphs where Ignatius describes three instances when he faced death. The first occurred at Manresa when a fever brought him to death's door. He was convinced that he was about to die.

> At that instant the thought came into his mind that he was numbered among the righteous, but this brought him so much distress that he tried everything to dismiss it and to dwell on his sins. He had more difficulty with that thought than with the fever, but no matter how much he toiled to overcome it, he was unable to do so. When the fever lessened and he was no longer in danger of death, he loudly cried out to certain

ladies who had come to visit him that the next time
they saw him at death's door they were, for the love
of God, to shout aloud that he was a sinner and that
he should be ever mindful of the sins he had commit-
ted against God.[80]

Contrast this experience with the next one he describes. He
was on ship from Spain to Italy and in a storm everyone on
board was convinced that death was inevitable.

Thus, making use of his time, he made a careful
examination of conscience and prepared himself for
death, but he felt no fear because of his sins nor was
he afraid of being condemned, but he was especially
disturbed and sorry, knowing that he had not put to
good use all the gifts and graces that God our Lord
had granted him.[81]

Now Ignatius knows that he is a sinner and that knowledge sad-
dens him, but it does not frighten him. He trusts in the mercy of
God. The self-God image seems to be that of a person who is
convinced that he is a sinner loved and forgiven by an all-merci-
ful God.

Then Ignatius describes a time in the year 1550 when he
and everyone else were convinced that he was about to die of a
fever:

Thinking of death at that time, he experienced such
joy and such spiritual consolation in the thought of
having to die that he burst into tears. This came to be
of such frequent occurrence that many times he
stopped thinking of death just so as not to have so
much consolation.[82]

Now Ignatius seems to be enamored of God, totally caught up

with the desire for ultimate union with God. Thoughts of his sins do not seem to arise. The self-God image seems to be that of beloved to lover. God has taught Ignatius the ultimate lesson of who God really is for Ignatius, and for all of us, Lover *par excellence*. Fidelity to the relationship with God has changed Ignatius' image of God as well as his image of himself.

Ignatius urges the one who directs the *Spiritual Exercises* to "allow the Creator to deal immediately with the creature and the creature with its Creator and Lord" (n. 15). In that encounter with God the retreatant can learn a new and more realistic self-God schema. All of us have schemata that impoverish our experience of God and, thus, of ourselves. In his *Autobiography* Ignatius shows himself as a pilgrim who moves from a small view of God to one of God as Lover. Ignatius believed that the same change can happen to us.

9

TOUCHSTONE EXPERIENCES AS DIVINING RODS IN DISCERNMENT

In *The Practice of Spiritual Direction* William Connolly and I describe how Ignatius of Loyola finally recognized the demonic origin of his "serpent" image after his illumination at the river Cardoner, a point we noted in the last chapter. We then note:

> Here we see one of the criteria that people use to decide whether an experience is of God: They compare it to another experience that they are sure is of God. Then, if they see that in some respect the two conflict, they decide which experience to accept. Many people have a touchstone experience of God. Any other experience that seems to run counter to that touchstone they look upon with suspicion. God can be so manifestly present to them during such a touchstone experience that they cannot doubt it any more than they can doubt their own existence.[83]

People may wonder what such experiences could be. I believe that the resurrection appearances of Jesus in the gospels illustrate the positive use of touchstone experiences to recognize the risen Lord. Reflection on some of these stories may help us to discover our own touchstone experiences and to help directees to discover theirs.

Mary Magdalene saw a stranger whom she took to be a gardener. Her own love for Jesus shows itself poignantly when the "gardener" asks her: "Woman, why are you weeping? Whom are you looking for?" "Sir, if you have carried him away, tell me where you have laid him, and I will take him away." Then the stranger said: "Mary." "She turned and said to him in Hebrew, 'Rabbouni!' (which means Teacher)" (Jn 20: 15–16). The familiar voice speaking her name instantly tells her that the stranger is her beloved Jesus.

The two disciples walking sadly toward Emmaus also met a stranger who spoke meaningfully about the scriptures and the suffering Messiah. Yet, though their hearts were burning as they walked along with him, they did not recognize him. Still they did not want to let him go when they reached their destination. Perhaps something was tugging at the sleeves of their memories. When they had prevailed on the stranger to stay for a meal with them, "he took bread, blessed and broke it, and gave it to them. Then their eyes were opened, and they recognized him" (Lk 24: 30–31). The familiar gesture of blessing bread and breaking and giving it, a gesture which before the crucifixion must have burned itself into their hearts as an archetypal experience of Jesus, lets them see in this stranger the Lord whose death had dashed all their hopes. Only now do they pay attention to the fact that their hearts were burning during the whole time the stranger was with them.

In the twenty-first chapter of John's gospel we read that Peter and the other disciples went fishing and caught nothing all night. In the morning a stranger told them: "Cast the net to the right side of the boat, and you will find some." "So they cast it, and now they were not able to haul it in because there were so many fish. That disciple whom Jesus loved said to Peter, "It is the Lord!" (Jn 21: 6–7). The gospel writer seems to be alluding to the miraculous catch of fish which, in the synoptic gospels, inaugurates the call of the disciples as apostles. Again a touchstone experience of Jesus is brought back to memory and leads to the recognition of the Lord in a new situation.

I suspect that many (most) people have such touchstone

experiences of God. In fact, social science research indicates that the majority of people, at least in the United States and Great Britain, have rather powerful experiences of God.[84] But I also suspect that most of us who do have such experiences do not give them enough credit. We do not pay enough attention to them and fix them in memory. As a result they are episodic events in our lives, like passing stomach aches, to which we pay little heed once they have passed. Hence, they cannot serve as the divining rods for the discernment of God's presence in new situations. I write this short chapter to encourage us to help people (and ourselves) to pay attention to the moments when they feel their hearts burning, as it were.

Perhaps just reading this chapter this will jog the reader's memory and bring back to mind an experience that was deeply felt and could serve as such a touchstone. On occasion it has happened to me that the very act of telling my spiritual director about an experience that had not seemed important sparks a memory of the experience that is even more powerful than the original. Some people I direct have come to realize that experiences that initially seemed minor were profound revelations of God as they described them in direction. Sometimes we need to be asked about experiences before we recognize how important they are to us. The Religious Experience Research Unit at Oxford University in England has received thousands of accounts of religious experiences since its founding in 1969 by putting ads in newspapers and through pamphlets. They asked readers to send in records of religious experiences they had had along with relevant personal information. Replies poured in from all over Britain. Many of them are striking and could be the touchstone experiences we have been discussing. A few examples from Alister Hardy's book will give the flavor.

> I heard nothing, yet it was as if I were *surrounded by golden light* and as if I only had to reach out my hand

to touch God himself who was so surrounding me with his compassion.[85]

It seemed to me that, in some way, I was extending into my surroundings and was becoming one with them. At the same time I felt a sense of lightness, exhilaration and power as if I was beginning to understand the true meaning of the whole universe.[86]

One night I suddenly had an experience as if I was buoyed up by waves of utterly sustaining power and love. The only words that came near to describing it were "underneath are the everlasting arms," though this sounds like a picture, and my experience was not a picture but a feeling, and there were the arms. This I am sure has affected my life as it has made me know the love and sustaining power of God. *It came from outside and unasked.*[87]

On the first night I knelt to say my prayers, which I had now made a constant practice, I was aware of a glowing light which seemed to envelop me and which was accompanied by a sense of warmth all round me.[88]

Suddenly I felt a great joyousness sweeping over me. I use the word "sweeping" because this feeling seemed to do just that. I actually felt it as coming from my left and sweeping round and through me, completely engulfing me. I do not know how to describe it. It was not like a wind. But suddenly it was there, and I felt it move around and through me. Great joy was in it. Exaltation might be a better word.[89]

Whether these experiences would have meant as much to the writers had they not been asked to send them to the Research Unit I do not know. However, I venture to say that the interest of the Unit in hearing about such experiences may well have

jogged the memories of some of the writers to recall the experiences and to savor them more deeply. Now they could be used
as the kind of touchstone for discerning new experiences of
God. However, they might need the help of another person like
a spiritual director to see the possibility of such use.

As indicated earlier, for St. Ignatius of Loyola the illumination at the river Cardoner seems to have been such a touchstone experience. In his autobiography he describes how he sat
down at the river:

> As he sat there the eyes of his understanding were
> opened and though he saw no vision he understood
> and perceived many things, numerous spiritual things
> as well as matters touching on faith and learning, and
> this was with an elucidation so bright that all these
> things seemed new to him. . .he received such a
> lucidity in understanding that during the course of his
> entire life—now having passed his sixty-second
> year—if he were to gather all the helps he received
> from God and everything he knew, and add them
> together, he does not think they would add up to all
> that he received on that one occasion.[90]

Not only does Ignatius emphasize how strong an impression this illumination made on him for the rest of his life, but
immediately after the experience he is able to discern that the
serpent-like vision which had formerly given him such comfort
was a temptation. The touchstone experience at the river
Cardoner enabled him to discern wheat from chaff in other
experiences.

Just as Mary and the other disciples recognized the
"stranger" as their risen Lord through some gesture that reminded them of a profound experience of Jesus, so too all of us can
use the memory of touchstone experiences of God to discern
whether our present experiences are of the same "stuff," as it

were. But we need to savor and nourish the memory of such experiences and tell them to our spiritual directors.

Telling one's spiritual director about such experiences can have two consequences. First, as noted earlier, the telling itself both etches the experience in memory and can help me to remember even more of the experience than I initially recalled. In the telling I remember details I had not paid attention to but which still made an impression on me. The disciples on the road to Emmaus only realized that their hearts had been burning within them throughout the journey with the stranger after the breaking of the bread. So, too, we often only realize the full impact of touchstone experiences after the fact and in the telling. Second, telling the spiritual director can have unintended and beneficial consequences for future spiritual direction sessions. Often enough in spiritual direction sessions I remember profound experiences that a directee has told me when the directee, because of desolation and/or resistance, does not remember them. I have, in many such instances, reminded the directee of the past experience of intense consolation, either to help the directee to resist the pull of profound desolation, or to help him/her to discern what is happening at the present moment and to decide which experience to trust. It sometimes happens that the desolation is a resistance reaction to experiences of profound intimacy with the Lord.[91] Remembering and telling about profound experiences of closeness to the Lord can be a royal road to an ever-deepening intimacy.

10

TOWARD COMMUNAL DISCERNMENT: SOME PRACTICAL SUGGESTIONS

Something interesting happened in the Society of Jesus between the 31st General Congregation (1965–66) and the 32nd (1974–75). Every reference to spiritual discernment or the discernment of spirits in the documents of G.C. 31 refers to individual discernment, whereas the preponderance of such references in G.C. 32 are to discernment in common. G.C. 31 is obviously concerned that the Society recover the dynamic of the *Spiritual Exercises* and especially the individual discernment of spirits. While not neglecting the need for such a continuing recovery G.C. 32 makes an effort to encourage communities to become communities of discernment.

> Clearly, the requisite dispositions for true communitarian discernment are such that they will not be verified as often as those for ordinary community dialogue. Nevertheless, every community should seek to acquire them, so that when need arises it can enter into this special way of seeking the will of God.[92]

What happened between 1966 and 1975?

In North America the directed retreat movement (giving the *Spiritual Exercises* individually) spread like a brush fire through the Society. At G.C. 31 it was almost timidly suggested: "The scholastics should be permitted on occasion during their formation to make the *Spiritual Exercises* alone under the direction of an experienced spiritual father..."[93] By the time of G.C.

32 hardly a scholastic in North America made the Exercises in any other way. Spiritual direction with an emphasis on the discussion of the actual religious experience of the directee also took on great importance.

But along with this increased interest in individual spiritual direction and this recovery of the original intention of St. Ignatius in giving the Exercises, also went a renewed interest in other aspects of Ignatian spirituality. The Institute of Jesuit Sources under George Ganss began publishing English translations of original Jesuit documents, the most important being the appearance in 1970 of Ganss' own translation of the *Constitutions*.[94] The Institute also made available in translation such scholarly works as de Guibert's *The Jesuits: Their Spiritual Doctrine and Practice*[95] and began publishing original studies that made it possible for English-speaking Jesuits to recover their spiritual heritage. Finally, in 1969 the American Assistancy Seminar on Jesuit Spirituality under the direction of George Ganss began publishing the very influential monograph series, *Studies in the Spirituality of Jesuits*. Thus, the Society in North America responded to the call of Vatican II and G.C. 31 that religious try to recover the charism of their founders.

Very early in the *Studies* series, in April, 1970, "Ignatian Discernment" by John Futrell appeared.[96] This monograph, based on Futrell's doctoral dissertation, focused not only on individual discernment but also on communal discernment modeled on the deliberation that led to the founding of the Society of Jesus. A year and a half later Jules Toner's "A Method for Communal Discernment"[97] appeared to be followed in November, 1972, by Futrell's "Communal Discernment: Reflections on Experience."[98] Finally, in June, 1974, Toner's "The Deliberation That Started the Jesuits"[99] made its appearance. Since that time nothing more on communal discernment has appeared in the *Studies* series.

Even a cursory reading of these four publications makes it clear that Futrell, Toner and other Jesuits were giving numerous workshops on communal discernment to groups of religious. During these same years William J. Connolly, S.J., of the Center for Religious Development in Cambridge, Massachusetts, was in demand to conduct similar workshops and introduced me to the process when together we facilitated such a workshop for all the Jesuit superiors of the New England province in 1972. In short order I was asked to facilitate a number of such workshops in New England and abroad. A stint as vice-provincial for formation took me out of circulation for such work until 1984 when, with Joseph McCormick, S.J., I was asked to work with the Jesuits of a large urban area to help them move toward communal discernment. What intrigues me is the silence about communal discernment since the surge of interest in the early 1970s which culminated in the call of G.C. 32. I suspect that attempts at communal discernment have foundered because the prerequisites were not present in groups.

Whenever I conducted a communal discernment workshop I kept detailed process notes on what went on. I want to describe the process as I saw it, with the hope that such a description will be helpful to others. If the process of communal discernment has, in fact, fallen into disuse, perhaps we need a stimulus to bring it back into use. In 1970 Futrell argued strongly that the times required a recovery of the Ignatian practice of communal discernment.

> If true communal discernment of experiments to enable the Society of Jesus to renew itself and to adapt to the signs of the times today is a condition for the survival of the Society in the modern Church, then it is vital that all Jesuits learn to engage in authentic Ignatian communal discernment.[100]

More than twenty years later, I believe the need is still there, and not just for Jesuits.

I have entitled the chapter "Toward Communal Discern-

ment" quite deliberately. Many of the workshops in which I
have participated have not reached the point of engaging in true
communal discernment, either because no question for discernment arose, or because of lack of time or because other things
needed to happen first. I suspect that many attempts at communal discernment falter for lack of the prerequisites outlined by
both Futrell (1970 and 1972) and Toner (1971). Since both of
these men have provided relatively detailed outlines of the actual process of discernment they use once these prerequisites are
attained, I want to concentrate on the process of moving toward
that attainment.

Communal discernment presupposes before all else that
those who will engage in it have experienced the discernment of
spirits in themselves. That is, each individual must have engaged
in a process of contemplative prayer such as that proposed in the
Spiritual Exercises and have experienced the movements of the
different "spirits" and have discerned which movements were of
God, which not. Secondly, communal discernment presupposes
that the individuals can and will communicate to others their
experiences in prayer and in prayerful reflection. The ability to
do so cannot be presupposed since many of us were brought up
in a tradition where such communication was not only not
encouraged but often enough actively discouraged. The recovery
of the individually directed retreat and the development of a type
of spiritual direction which requires the communication of religious experience are giving us the tools for the kind of communication communal discernment requires. But the willingness to
communicate experience must also be present, and this is often
the rock upon which attempts at communal discernment shatter.
Let me elaborate on this point.

When will any of us—unless we are inveterate narcis-
sists—reveal our intimate selves to others? Is it not when we
trust the other, trust the other not to laugh or scorn or downplay
our experience? Suppose that you start to tell me about an experience of prayer that meant something to you and I swiftly

change the subject or say: "That sounds odd to me." It will be a long time before you will take the chance again. When people approach a counselor for help because they are deeply troubled, they will test the waters with him or her before they reveal their intimate selves. And directees only gradually reveal the most intimate aspects of their relationship with God as they come to trust their spiritual directors. So it is not easy to entrust our inner experience to others.

If this is the case in one-to-one relationships, how much more difficult to reveal ourselves in a group. Very often our reluctance to reveal ourselves comes from fear. What follows is a description of some of the processes we have used to help people in groups to overcome their fears and to entrust themselves more to one another.

First we explain the role of the facilitators by an analogy to the role of the spiritual director. The spiritual director helps individuals to recognize their desires with regard to the Lord, to make these known to the Lord, and to put themselves into a receptive position so that the Lord's response may be heard. The spiritual director does not manufacture desires or prayer experiences for the directee, but helps the person to notice what is happening in the relationship with the Lord, to discern what leads toward the Lord, and to decide what to do about the discernment. So, too, the facilitators of the group try to help the group to articulate its desire as a group with regard to the Lord and to help them to approach the Lord in prayer with that desire. Here it is important to remind the individuals that they are asking the Lord to relate to them precisely as members of this group with the group's desire, e.g., to know that the Lord has hopes for *us* as a group. Just as individuals ask the Lord for what they desire, trusting that the Lord has their good at heart, so too the individuals in this group context approach the Lord with the group's desire trusting that the Lord has the good of this group at heart.

The facilitators suggest a way for the members to approach the Lord in personal prayer with the desire for the Lord's help precisely as a member of this group. After the prayer period is over, they return to the group. The facilitators then help them to report to one another as much or as little as they wish of what happened during the prayer. Just as the spiritual director of an individual helps the person to notice and articulate what happened as much as possible without judging it, so too the facilitators of a group ask the group to try to listen without judgment to the experiences shared. Indeed, since the assumption of such group sharing is that we are hoping to hear what God is saying to us as a group, these periods of sharing are approached, as far as possible, with the same contemplative attitude one hopes to have in private prayer.

Secondly, we point out that the process is a slow one of growing in trust in the Lord and in one another. They already trust the Lord, but they probably have not thought much about the Lord's desires and hopes for the group as such. And most groups need to develop a trust in one another as deeply prayerful and honestly searching for God's will for the group. Communal discernment means that each member of the group trusts that God will reveal his will for the group through their individual prayer and through their sharing of the fruits of that prayer. To engage in this process I must trust that all the others are sincerely praying and trying to remain open to discern God's will. After all, my future is on the line since I am willing to abide by the group's decision.

We have usually structured the day into three sessions, morning, afternoon and evening. The whole group gathers at the beginning of each session, and we give them some orientation for private prayer. Each one prays for forty-five minutes to an hour and then takes a few minutes for reflection. If the group is less than ten, all the sharing sessions are in one group. If it is larger, we break it up into groups of ten or less for the sharing and ask that someone summarize for the whole group in a report. Each session, therefore, lasts at least two and one-half hours. As the process goes on, we may have to vary the structure according to what is needed. For example, at the beginning of a session we may need to canvass the group to find out what their desires are.

Some groups begin the discernment process with much good will toward one another. Even so, the individuals will still need time to develop the deeper trust in one another and the Lord that this process entails. Suppose that such a group's purpose is to discover how they might best use their talent apostolically. Their numbers have declined and they feel strained and overworked and realize that they can no longer continue to do all the work that they have been doing. We would suggest for the first period of prayer that they use a text like Isaiah 43: 1–7:

> Do not fear, for I have redeemed you;
>> I have called you by name, you are mine.
> When you pass through the waters, I will be with you;
>> and through the rivers, they shall not overwhelm
>> you;
> when you walk through fire, you shall not be burned,
>> and the flame shall not consume you.
> For I am the Lord your God,
>> the Holy One of Israel, your Savior.
> Because you are precious in my eyes,
>> and honored, and I love you,
> I give people in return for you,
>> nations in exchange for your life.
> Do not fear, for I am with you.

We indicate that the Israelites heard these consoling words when they were in exile, their temple destroyed and their hopes at their lowest. We suggest that they ask the Lord to give them a sense of hearing these words as applying to them as members of this group.

They then pray privately for forty-five minutes or so, and afterwards return to the group where each one is asked to share whatever he or she wishes of what happened during the prayer. For most groups such an ice-breaker is reassuring and the variety of experiences enlightening. In a felt way they realize how sincere and faith-filled each one is. They are often surprised at how easy and enjoyable it is to talk about prayer with one another. Depending on how this first session goes, we might either suggest a repetition for the next session or suggest that they ask the Lord to help them to know his dreams for them as a group.

During the group meetings we remind them to listen to one another contemplatively and to note inner reactions as they listen. If they feel antipathy to what one member is saying, for example, they might want to ask the Lord's help to see things from that person's perspective. After the group has articulated its vision and dream as best it can, they might be ready to ask the Lord's help to discover what blocks them from realizing the dream. Now the hard part begins, because they will be addressing neuralgic issues that may bring to light resentments, mistrust, and other "negative" emotions. The facilitators now begin to earn their keep.

Any group that has a history together has got some bodies buried somewhere. We have been talking about groups who begin the process with much good will toward one another. Often enough, however, groups do not begin with much good will and trust. Then the negative feelings may have to be addressed even earlier.

One group displayed so much anger, resentment, suspicion, and misunderstanding at the very first session that even the facilitators wondered whether they had opened Pandora's box. But we pointed out that their reality had surfaced rather quickly, and suggested that they might feel as the apostles did after the crucifixion when they boarded themselves up in the upper room. Imagine their feelings of guilt and anger and suspicion and fear. And into their midst came Jesus saying, "Peace be with you." We suggested that they might want to spend an hour in prayer with this text (Jn 20: 19–23) and then return. When they returned to the group, the atmosphere had noticeably shifted. Where before accusations and angry denunciations of others prevailed, now each one spoke of his own fears and failings and at the same time voiced a trust that the Lord would be with them. We had not yet reached the promised land, but we were on the way toward becoming a group that eventually might be able to engage in communal discernment.

In his 1972 monograph, Futrell makes a perceptive comment: "A community must have achieved the fruit of the First Week of the *Spiritual Exercises as a community* in order to begin true communal spiritual discernment."[101] He does not spell out what that might mean, but I believe that this prerequisite is crucial, and in at least one case, I believe, I saw a group achieve that fruit. It was a group of male religious who were chapter delegates. They asked two of us to facilitate a four-and-a-half-day process that would help them toward being more discerning and open during the chapter which would follow. The congregation was reeling from a heavy financial blow and from departures that had left them demoralized, angry, and suspicious. Among the members of the group were some whom the others held responsible for their problems. Early in our sessions feelings of anger, suspicion, guilt, and helplessness emerged. The first two days were stormy, but we could sense a gradual growth in trust. As one man said: "We have thought the unthinkable and said the unsayable."

Toward the end of the second day we summarized the situation in this fashion. "You sense yourselves as broken, needy, helpless, and sinful precisely as members of this congregation and as chapter delegates. A number of you have identified with Simon the Pharisee who scorned Jesus for letting the sinful woman wash his feet. Some of you have voiced resentment at being put into the position of picking up the pieces of a mess caused by others. Some have voiced fears that as a group you will not have the courage to make the necessary decisions. Some fear that even God cannot change you. And yet you have also desired healing, have desired that Jesus make you brothers again. We suggest that you present yourselves to Jesus as you are and ask him for what you want. Perhaps you might want to do a repetition of Luke 7: 36–50 or you might want to use the washing of the feet in John 13." We also suggested speaking to Jesus on the cross and using the triple colloquy of the First Week of the Exercises.

The sharing after this period of prayer was very emotional and very honest. One man asked with tears for the forgiveness of the group. Another reported emptiness in prayer and asked the group to pray for him. A couple of men said that the desire for healing was growing in them. Most of the others reported consolation and a sense of being healed. Tears were shed. At the end of the sharing they broke up into dyads for reconciliation. The next day men continued to ask one another for reconciliation. We spent the last two days focusing on Jesus' relationship with his apostles in the gospel of Mark. At the end of the process they felt hopeful and much more trusting as they prepared to enter their chapter. As a result of the "First Week experience" they seemed able to dream and to hope again as a group.

If spiritual directors need to have great trust in the Lord as their directees face some of the very painful and harrowing experiences sometimes associated with the process of conversion, it is even more imperative for those who facilitate groups toward communal discernment. It is all too easy to gloss over serious divisions in a group, to let sleeping dogs lie, as it were. It is all too easy to present techniques that only can work if prerequisites of trust and contemplative prayer are present. It is also all too easy to give up hope that the Lord can work his wonders even on a group that seems at first hopelessly divided. Perhaps they do want to be healed as a group. I have never been a facilitator alone, precisely because I feel the need for another, so that together we can remind one another to pray ourselves and to entrust the group to the Lord, and to trust the good will of the group in spite of everything. After all, we try to say to one another, they have invited us to help them to become a discerning group; so they must have some hope in the Lord who has called them together. A group is close to becoming discerning when the members can say, as one man did, "During the Spiritual Exercises I came to trust deeply that Jesus had a dream for me. Now I believe that he has a dream for us."

11

THE CONTEMPLATION TO OBTAIN LOVE

No one doubts that this contemplation is both "the conclusion and the apt climax of the spiritual experience of the Exercises."[102] What needs to be emphasized, however, is that this exercise is a contemplation, not a meditation. In other words, Ignatius does not expect that the fruit of this exercise will be attained by meditation or reflection on the four points in the manner of the First Week, using the intellect, memory and will to move oneself to the desired end. Rather, this exercise expects that retreatants will have arrived at the point where they desire experiences of God such that their hearts will be inflamed with a greater love of God "in all things." The desire of this contemplation is expressed this way: "to ask for interior knowledge of all the great good I have received, in order that, stirred to profound gratitude, I may become able to love and serve the Divine Majesty in all things" (n. 233). In the Second Week retreatants desired "interior knowledge" of Jesus, an interior knowledge that can only come if Jesus reveals himself to them; and this interior knowledge is expected to issue in greater love and service. So, too, in this exercise retreatants desire a revelation of God, "interior knowledge," such that their hearts will spontaneously be moved to love and service. Let me spell out the implications of this contemplation as I see them.

It lies close to hand to see the text of this contemplation as the fruit of Ignatius' own mystical experiences at Manresa. He describes five of them in rapid succession in the *Autobiography*, beginning immediately after he has explained that "God was

dealing with him in the same way a schoolteacher deals with a
child while instructing him."[103]

> First....One day...his understanding was raised on
> high, so as to see the Most Holy Trinity under the
> aspect of three keys on a musical instrument, and as a
> result he shed many tears and sobbed so strongly that
> he could not control himself....This experience
> remained with him for the rest of his life so that
> whenever he prayed to the Most Holy Trinity he felt
> great devotion.[104]
>
> Second. One day it was granted him to understand,
> with great spiritual joy, the way in which God had
> created the world. He seemed to see a white object
> with rays stemming from it, from which God made
> light.[105]
>
> Third....One day, while in town attending Mass..., he
> saw with inward eyes, at the time of the elevation of
> the body of the Lord, some white rays coming from
> above...he clearly saw with his understanding how
> our Lord Jesus Christ was present in that most holy
> Sacrament.[106]
>
> Fourth. During prayer he often, and for an extended
> period of time, saw with inward eyes the humanity of
> Christ, whose form appeared to him as a white body,
> neither very large nor very small; nor did he see any
> differentiation of members...These things that he saw
> at that time fortified him and gave such great support
> to his faith that many times he thought to himself: if
> there were no Scriptures . . ., he would still resolve to
> die for them on the basis of what he had seen.[107]
>
> Fifth. [Facing the river Cardoner]...the eyes of his
> understanding were opened and though he saw no
> vision he understood and perceived many things,
> numerous spiritual things as well as matters touching

on faith and learning, and this with an elucidation so
bright that all these things seemed new to him.[108]

When Ignatius had these experiences, he was still a novice
in the spiritual life; moreover, he was practically innocent of any
theological knowledge. By the time retreatants come to the
Contemplation to Attain Love Ignatius expects that they will
have the desire for such personal revelations of God. They ask
for an "interior knowledge." Ignatius, it seems, does not believe
that he was singled out for the revelations he received because
of any merit of his; everything he received he considered a gift,
and a gift that others could also desire of God. Ignatius expects
that anyone can ask God for such a revelation and then hope that
God will respond.

The four points of the Contemplation recapitulate the interior meaning of the Principle and Foundation. The retreatant
now wants such a felt knowledge of the uniqueness of God and
of God's intention in creation, that it will be second nature to
live in a spirit of gratitude and in tune with God's intention for
the universe. Directors need to stress that these points are not so
much for meditation as openings to contemplation, as ways to
make oneself ready for divine revelation. Let retreatants note
well the two preliminary observations. "First. Love ought to
manifest itself more by deeds than by words" (n. 230). As we
noted earlier, following Egan, the mysticism of Ignatius is a servant mysticism, a mysticism of action in tune with the one
action of God.[109] Even this Contemplation to Obtain Love does
not deviate from this perspective. "Second. Love consists in a
mutual communication between the two persons" (n. 231). What
is extraordinary in this statement, and what follows it, is the
mutuality which Ignatius presupposes that God wants. God, by
free choice, depends on our free choice to be who God wants to
be for us. If we do not choose to respond in mutuality, then God
cannot be for us who God wants to be, namely, one who com-
municates in mutuality.

In the first point I ask to remember with deep affection all the gifts I have received both as part of the universe and the human race and as a particular individual with a particular history. This point recalls our reference to asking God to reveal to us our personal salvation history in the chapter on the Principle and Foundation. Moreover, Ignatius notes how much God "desires to give me even his very self, in accordance with his divine design" (n. 234). To the extent that we experience such divine love and let it penetrate our hearts, to that extent we will want to say with all our hearts, "Lord, I want to give you all that I am in return." Ignatius expresses it in his justly famous prayer:

> Take, Lord, and receive all my liberty, my memory, my understanding, and all my will—all that I have and possess. You, Lord, have given all that to me. I now give it back to you, O Lord. All of it is yours. Dispose of it according to your will. Give me love of yourself along with your grace, for that is enough for me (n. 234).

Someone in the throes of such love has no fear to tell God anything or to entrust God with all one's life and hopes and aspirations. He or she will "desire and choose only what is more conducive to the end for which we are created" (n. 23).

In the second point I ask to experience "how God dwells in creatures...; and finally, how in this way he dwells also in myself, giving me existence, life, sensation, and intelligence; and even further, making me his temple..." (n. 235). If we have a deep experience of God's divine indwelling in all things, then we will indeed find God in all things and tend to reverence all things and people and ourselves. One who has such a deep experience will never want to misuse any creature or oneself.

In the third point I ask to experience "how God labors and works for me in all the creatures on the face of the earth..."(n. 236). If God does reveal Godself so personally to me, then I will have an experience of God's one action in creating and sustaining the universe and will want with all my heart to live in tune with that one action. Macmurray's philosophy of action finds an echo in this point.

Finally, in the fourth point I ask to experience "how all good things and gifts descend from above...just as the rays come down from the sun, or the rains from their source" (n. 237). Here we see a clear echo of Ignatius' own mystical experiences as he described them in the *Autobiography*. If we could only experience all blessings and gifts as descending to us from above, then we would be able to live in spiritual poverty. We would be "indifferent to," "at balance toward," all created gifts and blessings because we would have intimate knowledge that these are only pale, even though wonderful, reflections of the One "from whom all blessings flow," the One who is the deepest desire of our hearts.

Thus, retreatants who come to this climax of the *Spiritual Exercises* come full circle. But now they know more intimately the Mystery we call God, and in the process know more intimately themselves and their world. They are well on the way to being contemplatives in action, people who find God regularly in their actual lives of prayer and action. Indeed, for such people prayer and action are not two different activities, but in some mysterious fashion one.

Notes

[1] Gilles Cusson, *Biblical Theology and the Spiritual Exercises: A Method toward a Personal Experience of God as Accomplishing within Us His Plan of Salvation.* Tr. Mary Angela Roduit and George E. Ganss. St. Louis, MO: The Institute of Jesuit Sources, 1988, 80.

[2] Harvey Egan notes that Ignatius has a service mysticism, not a bridal mysticism. His spirituality cannot rest in union with God or Jesus alone unless it is union in service. Cf. Harvey D. Egan, *Ignatius Loyola the Mystic.* Wilmington, DE: Michael Glazier, 1987.

[3] Henry Guntrip, *Psychotherapy and Religion.* New York: Harper, 1957, 194–195. The citation of Mackenzie is from *Nervous Disorders and Character.*

[4] Cited in Henry Guntrip, *op. cit.*, 194–195. Of course, Ignatius would not agree that such enjoyment of God is the supreme end of spiritual technique. For him consolation had an orientation to action in accordance with God's will.

[5] Cf. Sebastian Moore, *Let This Mind Be in You: The Quest for Identity through Oedipus to Christ.* San Francisco: Harper & Row (Winston), 1985.

[6] Cf. C. S. Lewis, *Surprised by Joy: The Shape of My Early Life.* London: Geoffrey Bles, 1955.

[7] C. S. Lewis, *The Pilgrim's Regress: An Allegorical Apology for Christianity, Reason and Romanticism.* New York: Sheed & Ward, 1944, 7–10.

[8] In a recent monograph Joseph Tetlow draws similar conclusions. Cf. "The Fundamentum: Creation in the Principle and Foundation," *Studies in the Spirituality of Jesuits* 21, no. 4 (September, 1989). "When I talk about creation here, I have in mind the *In principio* of John's prologue and the first chapter of Ephesians. Hence, I mean a different beginning, a beginning in no way limited by time or place but always ongoing in specific time and concrete place. When I talk about creation in these pages, I refer to God's constantly making each creature out of nothing at each moment of its existence, anteceding and causing all secondary causes" (4–5). We shall deal more with the Principle in chapter 4.

[9] There is an analogy here to the developmental stages of Erik H. Erikson and of others. Cf. Erik H. Erikson, *Childhood and Society* (2nd. ed. New York: Norton, 1963) and for psychologists more influenced by Piaget, cf. Elizabeth Ann Liebert, *The Developmental Context of Spiritual Direction* (New York/ Mahwah: Paulist, 1992).

[10] For a helpful introduction to such counseling skills, cf. Gerard Egan, *The Skilled Helper: A Systematic Approach to Effective Helping.* 3rd ed. (Belmont, CA: Brooks/Cole, 1986). For a further development of this approach to spiritual direction cf. William A. Barry and William J. Connolly, *The Practice of Spiritual Direction* (San Francisco: Harper & Row, 1982).

[11] Leo Bakker, *Freiheit und Erfahrung: Redaktionsgeschichtliche Untersuchungen über die Unterscheidung der Geister bei Ignatius von Loyola* (Würzburg: Echter Verlag, 1970), 255, (translation mine). Harvey D. Egan makes a similiar point in *The Spiritual Exercises and the Ignatian Mystical Horizon* (St. Louis, MO: Institute of Jesuit Sources, 1976).

[12] I am citing Gerard Manley Hopkins' poem "God's Grandeur."

[13] Cf. William A. Barry and William J. Connolly, *op. cit,* chapter 11.

[14] Sebastian Moore, *Let This Mind Be in You: The Quest for Identity through Oedipus to Christ.* Minneapolis: Winston-Seabury, 1985.

[15] In another context I have discussed the courage of Bartimaeus. Cf. "Surrender: Key to Wholeness," in *Paying Attention to God: Discernment in Prayer.* Notre Dame, IN: Ave Maria, 1990, chapter 6.

[16] Joseph A. Tetlow, "The Fundamentum: Creation in the Principle and Foundation," *Studies in the Spirituality of Jesuits,* 21/4 (September 1989).

[17] *Ibid.*, 7.

[18] In the section which follows I borrow liberally from chapter 2 of my book *Finding God in All Things: A Companion to the Spiritual Exercises of St. Ignatius.* Notre Dame, IN: Ave Maria Press, 1991.

[19] Sebastian Moore, *Let This Mind Be in You: The Quest for Identity through Oedipus to Christ. Minneapolis,* Chicago, New York: Winston, 1985, 36.

[20] C. S. Lewis, *Surprised by Joy: The Shape of My Early Life.* London: Geoffrey Bles, 1955, 22.

[21] Frederick Buechner, *The Sacred Journey.* San Francisco: Harper & Row, 1965, 52.

[22] Ibid., 56.

[23] Anne Tyler, *Dinner at the Homesick Restaurant.* New York: Berkley Books, 1983, 284.

[24] C. S. Lewis, *The Pilgrim's Regress: An Allegorical Apology for Christianity, Reason and Romanticism.* New York: Sheed & Ward, 1944, 7–10.

[25] I develop the thought of John Macmurray and apply it to the encounter with God and spiritual direction in *Spiritual Direction and the Encounter with God: A Theological Inquiry.* New York/Mahwah: Paulist, 1992.

[26] Tetlow, "The Fundamentum," *op. cit.* 8–9.

[27] George E. Ganss, *The Spiritual Exercises of Saint Ignatius: A Translation and Commentary.* St. Louis, MO: The Institute of Jesuit Sources, 1992, 151.

[28] Roger Haight, S.J., *Dynamics of Theology.* New York/Mahwah: Paulist, 1990, 153.

[29] *Ibid.*, 156–157.

[30] Cf. Gerald G. May, *Addiction and Grace.* San Francisco: Harper & Row, 1988.

[31] Cited in chapter 1 and quoted in Henry Guntrip, *Psychotherapy and Religion* (New York: Harper, 1957), 194–195.

[32] Cf. Joseph N. Tylenda, *A Pilgrim's Journey: The Autobiography of Ignatius of Loyola.* Wilmington, DE: Michael Glazier, 1985, n. 24.

[33] For this insight I am indebted to William J. Connolly, S.J.

[34] John Macmurray, *Persons in Relation.* Atlantic Highlands, NJ: Humanities Press, 1979, 171.

[35] Cf. Edward E. Jones, Amerigo Farina, Albert H. Hastorf, Hazel Markus, Dale T. Miller, and Robert Scott, *Social Stigma: The Psychology of Marked Relationships.* New York: Freeman, 1984.

[36] Ernest Becker, *The Denial of Death.* New York: Free Press, 1973.

[37] From my own *Finding God in All Things: A Companion to the Spiritual Exercises of St. Ignatius.* Notre Dame, In: Ave Maria, 1991, 124–125.

[38] John Macmurray, *Persons in Relation.* Atlantic Highlands, NJ: Humanities Press, 1979, 171.

[39] Cf. Barry, *Finding God in All Things, op. cit.,* 127–128.

[40] Joseph N. Tylenda, *A Pilgrim's Journey: The Autobiography of Ignatius of Loyola.* Wilmington, DE: Michael Glazier, 1985, n. 8.

[41] The Jesuit psychoanalyst William W. Meissner, in his psychobiography *Ignatius of Loyola: The Psychology of a Saint* (New Haven: Yale, 1992), shows rather convincingly that God's grace built on the psychic structure of Ignatius and that this psychic structure never disappeared.

[42] Cf. M. Basil Pennington, *Centering Prayer: Renewing an Ancient Christian Prayer Form.* Garden City, NY: Doubleday, 1980.

[43] Cf. John Main, *The Heart of Creation.* London: Darton, Longman and Todd, 1988.

[44] For a description of the kind of spiritual direction needed, cf. William A. Barry and William J. Connolly, *The Practice of Spiritual Direction.* San Francisco: Harper & Row-Seabury, 1982.

[45] Tylenda, *op. cit.,* nn. 15–16.

[46] John Macmurray, *Freedom in the Modern World.* London: Faber & Faber, 1968.

[47] Cf. William A. Barry, *Spiritual Direction and the Encounter with God: A Theological Inquiry*. New York and Mahwah: Paulist, 1992, chapter 6.

[48] Tylenda, *op. cit.*, n. 45.

[49] *Ibid.*, n. 47.

[50] Cf. Leo Bakker, *Freiheit und Erfahrung: Redaktions- geschichtliche Untersuchungen über die Unterscheidung der Geister bei Ignatius von Loyola.* Würzburg: Echter Verlag, 1970.

[51] Cf. Joseph A. Tetlow, "The Fundamentum: Creation in the Principle and Foundation," *Studies in the Spirituality of Jesuits* 21, no. 4 (September, 1989).

[52] Cf. John Macmurray, *The Self as Agent* and *Persons in Relation.* Atlantic Highlands, NJ: Humanities Press, 1978 and 1979. These two volumes contain the Gifford Lectures delivered in 1953–54.

[53] William A. Barry, *Spiritual Direction and the Encounter with God: A Theological Inquiry.* New York/Mahwah: Paulist, 1992, 22.

[54] William A. Barry, "The Kingdom of God and Discernment," in *Paying Attention to God: Discernment in Prayer.* Notre Dame, IN: Ave Maria Press, 1990, 77–85.

[55] Bakker, *op. cit.,* 105 (translation mine). In a recent article João MacDowell makes the same point: "Ignatius gives a second function to consolation/desolation, thus making an original and inestimable contribution to Christian spirituality. He uses them (consolation/desolation) as elements for the discernment of the movements of the spirits and, through such discernment, for the discovery of the will of God in my regard: election." João A. MacDowell, "Nota Sobre as Noções de 'Moção', 'Consolação' et 'Desolação' nos Exercícios Espirituais," *Itaici: Cadernos de Espiritualidade Inaciana,* 1 (1989), 51 (translation mine).

[56] For a more extensive development of these ideas, cf. William A. Barry, *Spiritual Direction and the Encounter with God: A Theological Inquiry, op. cit.*

[57] Tylenda, *op. cit.,* n. 26.

[58] *Ibid.*, n 55; n. 82.

[59] This is the felicitous phrase of George Aschenbrenner and far better expresses what Ignatius was about than the term "examination of conscience." Cf. George A. Aschenbrenner, "Consciousness Examen," *Review for Religious*, 31 (1972), 14–21. (Reprinted in David L. Fleming, ed., *Notes on the Spiritual Exercises of St. Ignatius of Loyola.* St. Louis: Review for Religious, 1983, 175–185.)

[60] William A. Barry, *Spiritual Direction and the Encounter with God,* chapter 6.

[61] William A. Barry, *Spiritual Direction and the Encounter with God, op. cit.,* 78.

[62] Josef Sudbrack, "Unterscheidung der Geister— Unterscheidung im Geiste," in Kurt Niederwimmer, Josef Sudbrack and Wilhelm Schmidt, *Unterscheidung der Geister: Skizzen zu einer neu zu lernenden Theologie des Heiligen Geistes.* Kassel: Johannes Stauda Verlag, 1972, 48.

[63] Susan Howatch, *Glamorous Powers.* New York: Fawcett Crest, 1988, 57–58.

[64] William A. Barry, *Spiritual Direction and the Encounter with God, op. cit.,* chapter 5.

[65] For an application of this theory to the relationship with God, cf. William A. Barry and William J. Connolly, *The Practice of Spiritual Direction, op. cit.,* chapter 6.

[66] Cf. Ana-Maria Rizzuto, *Birth of the Living God: A Psychoanalytic Study*. Chicago: University of Chicago Press, 1979.

[67] Tylenda, *A Pilgrim's Journey, op. cit.*, n. 8.

[68] *Ibid.*, n. 15.

[69] *Ibid.*, n. 12. (Italics mine.)

[70] *Ibid.*, n. 19.

[71] *Ibid.*, n. 19.

[72] *Ibid.*, n. 20.

[73] *Ibid.*, n. 23–24.

[74] Quoted in Henry Guntrip, *Psychotherapy and Religion*. New York: Harper, 1957, 195.

[75] Tylenda, *op. cit.*, n. 23.

[76] *Ibid.*, n. 25.

[77] *Ibid.*, n. 25.

[78] *Ibid.*, n. 26.

[79] *Ibid.*

[80] *Ibid.*, n. 32.

[81] *Ibid.*, n. 33.

[82] *Ibid.*

[83] William A. Barry and William J. Connolly, *The Practice of Spiritual Direction, op. cit.*, 103–4.

[84] Andrew M. Greeley reports that well over half of his respondents admit to having had memorable religious experiences. Cf. *The Religious Imagination.* New York: Sadlier, 1981. In Great Britain, Alister Hardy's Religious Experience Research Unit at Oxford University has received thousands of examples of memorable religious experiences. Cf. Alister Hardy, *The Spiritual Nature of Man: A Study of Contemporary Religious Experience.* Oxford: Clarendon Press, 1979.

[85] Hardy, *op. cit.,* 20.

[86] *Ibid.,* 21.

[87] *Ibid.,* 76–77 (italics mine).

[88] *Ibid.,* 34.

[89] *Ibid.,* 57.

[90] Tylenda, *op. cit.,* n. 30.

[91] Cf. William A. Barry, *Paying Attention to God: Discernment in Prayer* (Notre Dame, IN: Ave Maria Press, 1990), chapters 4, 5 and 6 for a discussion of resistance to positive experiences of God.

[92] Decree 11, "The Union of Minds and Hearts," of the 32nd General Congregation, para. 23. In *Documents of the 31st and 32nd General Congregations of the Society of Jesus* St. Louis, MO: The Institute of Jesuit Sources, 1977, 475.

[93] Decree 8, "The Spiritual Formation of Jesuits," of the 31st General Congregation, para. 124. In *Ibid.,* 108.

[94] Ignatius of Loyola, *The Constitutions of the Society of Jesus.* Tr. George E. Ganss. St. Louis, MO: The Institute of Jesuit Sources, 1970.

[95] Joseph de Guibert, *The Jesuits: Their Spiritual Doctrine and Practice. A Historical Study.* Tr. W. J. Young. St. Louis, MO: The Institute of Jesuit Sources, 1964.

[96] John C. Futrell, "Ignatian Discernment," *Studies in the Spirituality of Jesuits*, 2/2 (April, 1970).

[97] Jules J. Toner, "A Method of Communal Discernment of God's Will," *Studies in the Spirituality of Jesuits*, 3/4 (Sept., 1971).

[98] John C. Futrell, "Communal Discernment: Reflections on Experience," *Studies in the Spirituality of Jesuits*, 4/5 (Nov., 1972).

[99] Jules J. Toner, "The Deliberation That Started the Jesuits: A Commentary on the *Deliberatio primorum Patrum*. Newly Translated with a Historical Introduction," *Studies in the Spirituality of Jesuits*, 6/4 (June, 1974).

[100] Futrell, *op. cit.*, 1970, 70.

[101] Futrell, *op. cit.*, 1972, 169.

[102] George E. Ganss, *The Spiritual Exercises of Saint Ignatius*, *op. cit.*, 183, n.117.

[103] Tylenda, *Autobiography, op. cit.*, n. 27.

[104] *Ibid.*, n. 28.

[105] *Ibid.*, n. 29.

[106] *Ibid.*, n. 29.

[107] *Ibid.*, n. 29.

[108] *Ibid.*, n. 30.

[109] Cf. Harvey D. Egan, *Ignatius Loyola the Mystic*. Wilmington, DE: Michael Glazier, 1987.